*Is it not said
in all the old stories
that He is not
a Tame Lion?*

C. S. Lewis, **The Last Battle**

PROPHECY

JOEL B. GREEN

InterVarsity Press
Downers Grove
Illinois 60515

InterVarsity Press is the book-publishing division of Inter-Varsity Christian Fellowship, a student movement active on campus at hundreds of universities, colleges and schools of nursing. For information about local and regional activities, write IVCF, 233 Langdon St., Madison, WI 53703.

Quotations from Scripture in most instances are taken from the Holy Bible: New International Version. *Copyright © 1978 by the New York International Bible Society. Used by permission of Zondervan Bible Publishers. In instances where the translation differs from the NIV, it is the author's own rendering from the original language.*

Distributed in Canada through InterVarsity Press, 860 Denison St., Unit 3, Markham, Ontario L3R 4H1, Canada.

Cover illustration: Roberta Polfus

ISBN 0-87784-936-6

Printed in the United States of America

Library of Congress Cataloging in Publication Data
Green, Joel B., 1956-
    How to read prophecy.

    Includes bibliographies.
        1. Bible–Prophecies.   *2. Bible–Hermeneutics.*
I. Title.
BS647.2.G73   1984   *220.1'5*   *84-12838*
ISBN 0-87784-936-6 (pbk.)

15   14   13   12   11   10   9   8   7   6   5   4   3   2
95   94   93   92   91   90   89   88   87   86   85

THE HOW TO READ SERIES

The Bible is one book, yet it consists of many—history and wisdom, prophecy and apocalyptic, poetry and letters, law and narrative. This variety, while it enriches us, also challenges us. How are we to comprehend the unique contribution each type of literature makes to our understanding of God and our world?

The How to Read series is designed for nonprofessionals who want a professional understanding of Scripture. Each volume is written by an expert and focuses on one type of biblical literature, explaining its unique features and how these features should shape the way we approach it. The goal throughout is to help us all better understand the Bible and apply it to our lives.

To Aslan
My Hero!

Preface

Within the Christian church, few issues have received more heated attention than how to properly understand prophecy in the Bible. Indeed, the person who dares to enter this debate in the form of a published book may be guilty of the greatest folly, for dissenting voices are certain to come from the right and the left. When I first began to test the troubled waters of Joel, Daniel, John and the rest, the idea of presenting these thoughts before a wider audience was the furthest thing from my mind. That some of this material, presented in more primitive form to a number of classes and conferences, has finally reached this stage of redaction is only a sign of the many questions related to biblical prophecy among modern Christians and of God's ability to use a not-so-willing servant.

In presenting these principles for interpreting the prophetic and apocalyptic Scriptures, I have tried to be sensitive to the issues raised by more popular treatments of the subject and to the currents of contemporary biblical scholarship. In keeping with this endeavor, I have included a glossary and suggested reading list at the close of the book. In the majority of instances, biblical quotations follow the New International Version, though at some points I have provided my own translation.

It is both a necessity and privilege to record my appreciation to the churches, classes and many friends who have patiently interacted with me on some of the issues presented in this study. My gratitude is especially extended to my friend Richard Dunagin, who willingly read this material in an earlier draft and suggested a number of important revisions; to Mike Walker, who first encouraged me to develop more systematically my thoughts on this subject and whose friendship is a continuing source of encouragement; and to IVP's Joan Lloyd Guest, who has proved to be a valuable friend and model of Christian charity in the process of preparing this book for publication. My wife, Pam, patiently listened to and interacted with this material at various stages in its development. To her and to our son, Aaron (whose birth coincided with the conception of this book), who endured the sacrifice of time necessary for completing the manuscript, I owe my greatest debt of love and gratitude.

1
Can We Understand Biblical Prophecy?

Autumn, 1975. Texas Tech University, Lubbock. I was a college sophomore. The sun-baked days were reminiscent of July or August, but the mood was very much back-to-school. Yet an air of expectancy pervaded the Christian community: The Billy Graham Crusade was coming to town, bringing with it spiritual refreshment and, for many of us, a break from the rigors of academia.

I dove headfirst into the whole affair, training as a counselor and rehearsing for the choir. The much-anticipated opening night finally arrived. I was busily preparing to make my way to Jones Stadium, where throngs of people would soon congregate, when there was a knock at the door. Kevin, a friend from another town, had come early for the crusade and stopped by for a chat. I was pulling on my boots when he suddenly perked up, remembering his exciting news: "Joel, the Lord's coming back!"

I looked up and, seeing the anticipation written across his

face, replied, "Yes. Amen. Maranatha."

"No, you don't understand," he went on. "This week. By this Saturday. Jesus returns sometime *this* week!"

I motioned at my watch—it was time to be off. We headed for the door. "Look, Kevin, I know Jesus is coming back, but don't start specifying dates. You know what the Bible says . . . "

What the Bible says, of course, is that no one knows the day or the hour of Jesus' return. Apparently Kevin had noted that passage carefully. "Yes, I know what the Bible says. But remember, I didn't say what *time* or even which *day*—I just said sometime this week!"

"Kevin," I whined.

"I know. I know. I was skeptical too," he inserted quickly. "But I heard this tape. It was really convincing—right on target. It was *so* scriptural! Say, I know—I'll bring it tomorrow night. Then you can listen to it. I'm sure you'll agree with it."

I was not sure how to take that last comment. I was sure, however, that I had no time (or desire) to listen to that tape—on top of classes, papers, exams *and* Billy Graham. So I played my trump card: "Yes, do bring the tape. I'll listen to it on Sunday." Catching his look of disgust, I countered, "After all, if Jesus does come back this week, what better place to be than a Graham Crusade?"

At the age of nineteen I was already a cynic about predictions of the end times. Several years before, Hal Lindsey and company had penetrated our rural community with *The Late Great Planet Earth* and a horde of tapes (You've just got to listen to this one!) which seemed to appear out of nowhere. I even possessed a bona fide Bible Map of Last-Day Events, given me by street evangelists at the State Fair of Texas. With these tools in hand I was fast becoming an expert on how Bible prophecy all hangs together, down to the most minute detail.

Alas, my "conversion" was not to be completed. The further I went, the more difficult it became to make it all fit. The more

I read the biblical prophets and the less I read the current books about prophecy, the less I understood and the more confused I became. Some biblical texts simply refused to be funneled into the preplanned schema that I had taken for truth.

Gradually I grew apathetic about prophecy. When asked about the rapture or Armageddon or the beast, I pleaded ignorance. As for the antichrist and the millennium, I was agnostic. Sure, the Lord was coming back, but who could say when? Pragmatist that I was, I forsook thoughts of the future in favor of more present-day concerns—like growing Christians, living in the presence of the Spirit, building relationships and so on. For me discussions of the future were a thing of the past.

Much against my design and good sense, a few years later I finally gave in to the insistence of a young adult fellowship to lead a study on Revelation and prophecy. As a result of that fresh interaction with biblical prophecy, I began to see how parochial my perspective on the faith had become. I was dismayed to discover how I had amputated discipleship from its significant context in the totality of God's purpose. New colors and texture were added to the mural of my understanding of God and life with him.

My pilgrimage could be diagrammed in circular fashion—to describe how I returned, finally, to belief in the import of prophecy. If so, I hope I have come home with a greater maturity in understanding and practicing biblical interpretation as well as with a deeper humility in presenting that interpretation.

The large number of Christian books discussing "things to come" currently on the market shows the widespread desire to know what the Bible has to say about these days and our future. I am sure I am not the only person left unsatisfied by all of this writing. I believe there are many persons like me for whom the many discussions on biblical prophecy have left more questions than answers. And I imagine I am not the only one to have been frustrated by the conflicting explanations offered by the so-called experts on the subject. Consequently, I am convinced that people need aids for unraveling the tangles of prophetic language, principles for interpreting the prophetic message. This book is an invitation, directed particularly to a nonscholarly audience, for Christians to learn how to read biblical prophecy for themselves.

2
Survey of Approaches to Interpretation

Central to the faith of the early church was its conviction that Jesus was the fulfillment of Old Testament prophecy and its belief that he would soon return to establish his kingdom. A few examples illustrate this point.[1] In Acts 13 Paul is reported to have been asked to speak in a Jewish synagogue at Pisidian Antioch. He responds by surveying a number of high points of Israel's history and then showing that this history reached its culmination in Jesus. No less than eight times in this brief oration Paul either speaks of what God "promised" and "fulfilled" or draws directly on Old Testament testimony—all to demonstrate that Jesus was the fulfillment of God's saving purpose. In holding this view, Paul and other early believers followed the example set by Jesus himself, as illustrated in his conversation on the road to Emmaus:

"How foolish you are, and how slow of heart to believe all that the prophets have spoken! Did not the Christ have to

suffer these things and then enter his glory?" And beginning with Moses and all the Prophets, he explained to them
what was said in all the Scriptures concerning himself.
(Lk 24:25-27)
Similarly, Philip told the Ethiopian eunuch the good news
about Jesus beginning with the prophet Isaiah (Acts 8:26-39).

The hope of Jesus' return is likewise amply attested in the
New Testament.[2] The celebration of the Lord's Supper, a frequent aspect of the early church's life, anticipated Jesus' coming (see 1 Cor 11:26).[3] First Corinthians 16:22 holds another,
apparently universal, expression of the early anticipation of
Jesus' return—the Aramaic expression *Maranatha,* which
means "Our Lord, come!"[4] That the phrase (and thus the
hope it embodies) was widespread among early disciples is
suggested by its use here in a letter to Greek-speaking Christians. We might do the same with Latin *(et cetera, ad lib)* or
French *(r.s.v.p., bon voyage!)*—but only with foreign phrases
which are commonly understood.

Again, 1 Thessalonians 1:9-10 relates how the Thessalonian Christians "waited for God's Son from heaven."[5] Later,
this same letter makes additional references to Jesus' coming
(4:15-16; 5:1-3). The author of Hebrews writes of Christ's
second appearance (9:28), and 1 Peter 1:7 speaks of the future revealing of Jesus. These are only selected examples
among many references, explicit and implicit, to Jesus'
return.

The expectations of those first believers raise an important
question for the contemporary church: What role does biblical eschatology† serve in determining our own faith and life?
Are our congregations serving under the challenge of the
biblical prophets? Do we live in the hope to which writers like
John and Daniel testified? Are we motivated to mission
because of the inbreaking kingdom of God? Or is our belief

---

†*Eschatology* and several other technical terms are defined in the glossary at the back of this book.

concerning the end times expressed only when we recite the last two phrases of the Apostles' Creed?

Perspectives on Biblical Prophecy

The relation of eschatology to our faith and life is largely determined by our approach to the Bible, and especially to those parts of the Bible popularly known as "biblical prophecy." In the chapters to come we will distinguish different types of literature within this latter category. For now it is sufficient to note that the lessons we draw from those Scriptures are related to our interpretive point of reference. Unfortunately, there is no consensus about how to interpret the Bible in general[6] and biblical prophecy in particular.[7] Indeed, few issues have resulted in greater conflict and emotional name calling than that of *how* to make sense of biblical prophecy.

Generally, the various perspectives on how to study biblical prophecy can be cataloged under four headings, though clearly within each group there is some measure of diversity. We will look briefly at each of these modern interpretive methods before going on to discuss principles of interpreting biblical prophecy.

1. For mature audiences only. The Gospels, New Testament Epistles, Psalms and Proverbs—these often at least appear to be messages which can be grasped easily enough. But the Hebrew prophets, Daniel and Revelation—how obscure they seem! Turning to biblical prophecy from most other parts of the Bible provokes a reaction like that of many people entering a gallery of modern, abstract art: What is this stuff? And, even after receiving an explanation from one supposedly in the know, there follows only the raised eyebrow and noncommittal reply, "Oh, how interesting." In most churches—evangelical or otherwise—few sermons on Revelation or Daniel are ever heard. When texts are chosen from those two books, they are almost without fail from the earlier, "safe" chapters.

Among many Christians biblical prophecy is an unknown territory, the last frontier, to be explored only by experts. Consequently, most Christians neglect whole sections of the Bible or pass over them quickly in a read-through-the-Bible exercise.

Of course, this procedure has its problems. Most important, Christians who shy away from these parts of the Bible rob themselves of a vital message, a message inspired by the Holy Spirit. Moreover, they leave themselves as unguarded prey to any self-proclaimed expert who happens along to explain what is in their Bibles.

2. *Let's be literal!* Far removed from those who suspect that biblical prophecy is beyond the comprehension of most Christians are those who are confident that every detail can be understood, if only the correct method is used. Thus does Herman A. Hoyt argue

for a principle of interpretation that brings the meaning of the Bible within the grasp of the rank and file of the people of God. This principle clearly stated is that of taking the Scriptures in their literal and normal sense, understanding that this applies to the entire Bible. This means that the historical content of the Bible is to be taken literally; the doctrinal material is also to be interpreted in this way; the moral and spiritual information likewise follows this pattern; and the prophetic material is also to be understood in this way.[8]

This way of viewing the Scriptures is attractive, not least because it holds the promise that the Bible will easily give us its message, that little or no hard work is involved. The literal method says that the words of the Bible should be taken at face value. The Bible's words are clear, according to literalists, and its message is readily accessible. However, as we shall see, interpretation *is* always necessary and cannot be by-passed —and sometimes it *is* hard work.

We will look more closely at literal interpretation in the next two chapters. For now, a few questions can be raised: (1) *Should* all of the Bible be understood literally? That is, is it consistent with the writers' intentions to read all texts in a literal way? (2) *Can* all of the Bible be understood literally? Of course, all interpreters admit that the Bible does at times use figurative language. But do literalists go far enough in recognizing the various kinds of literature (literary genres) contained in the Old and New Testaments? (3) *Do* literalists themselves always interpret literally? Or do their interpretations betray tendencies toward spiritualizing or allegorizing?

Within this general sphere of literal interpretation are interpreters we might call *sensationalists*. These persons demand a literal interpretation of biblical prophecy, but with an eye fixed to today's headlines. For example, in one of his most recent books, Hal Lindsey points out in rapid succession twenty-one alarming developments signifying the hopelessness of our modern era—economically, militarily, politically and morally. Then he writes:

> These are but a few of the current trends causing tremendous interest and concern among students of the ancient Hebrew prophets. How these events fit into the prophetic pattern and what they point to for the future are the subjects of this book.

Finally, he sounds the sobering note: "The very destiny of mankind is at stake."[9]

Who could deny that our world is now at a critical point? Certainly we would not fault Lindsey simply for gathering together a list of current events (though one might take issue with the bias evident in the selection of those headlines). The real issue is this: In identifying specific world affairs in our own day as the fulfillment of biblical prophecy, does Lindsey use the Scriptures in a way consistent with their intended purpose? To this question we must return in later chapters.

3. Higher-critical skepticism. Many people hold biblical criticism at arm's length because of the posture given it by some of its more radical practitioners. The problem, however, lies not with historical study per se but with the underlying presuppositions often accompanying such study. In his critique of the historical-critical method, Howard Marshall sets out these faulty principles in simplified form:

(a) All historical statements are open to doubt. The historian must approach all the evidence in a sceptical frame of mind, and his results will only be probable and never certain. (b) We can and must work out what kind of things happened in the past by analogy with our own experience in the present time. All events are in principle similar. (c) Everything, but everything, that happens in history is governed by the laws of natural cause and effect. Miracles and acts of God are impossible.[10]

Thus the assumptions of many higher critics make <u>predictive</u> <u>prophecy</u> unthinkable. Stated simply, the possibility of an accurate prediction is categorically ruled out of court. For example, Luke's Gospel records Jesus' prediction on different occasions of the devastation of Jerusalem (21:20-24; see also 19:41-44; 23:28-31). Because these words so closely parallel the actual events of the fall of Jerusalem in A.D. 70, a number of interpreters judge that Luke has reworked his tradition in light of the actual event. In its barest form this kind of argument is nothing more than prejudice.

Moreover, persons who interpret from the faulty presuppositions of higher criticism assert that <u>age-old biblical messages are</u> restricted to their original historical contexts. Biblical texts have value for modern readers as primary source material for historical investigation, but they were not intended as messages for our lives. As we shall see, <u>there is a</u> <u>measure of truth in this position: the biblical texts were written</u> <u>for particular, historical audiences, and we would do well</u> <u>to understand the Scriptures in their own setting</u>. Nevertheless, the historical message is <u>*not*</u> the whole story; <u>as divine</u> <u>words those biblical texts transcend the boundaries of their</u>

historical settings. This bare assertion will be worked out in fuller detail in chapter four.

4. Attention to literature and history. Often referred to as the grammatico-historical method of interpretation, this approach strives to take seriously matters of literary and historical import. This method recognizes that different parts of the Bible are cast in different kinds of literary genre—some poetic, some parabolic, some historical, and so on. In the preface to his study on Revelation, Robert H. Mounce aptly notes: "A critical problem facing every writer on the book of Revelation grows out of the literary genre in which the book is cast. . . . What kind of literature we are dealing with is the essential question."[11] This is true not only for the book of Revelation but for all biblical prophecy.

The grammatico-historical method is sensitive to the meaning of the biblical text in its historical setting. Today the idea of biblical prophecy suggests to many people that the words of the ancient prophets were given as predictions for our own day and carried no meaning for their original audiences. Attention to the historical setting of the prophecies, and to the intentions of the prophets themselves, corrects such misunderstanding.

Most books on biblical prophecy available today are based either on the literal method of interpretation or on the grammatico-historical approach. As we discuss how biblical prophecy is best understood, we will occasionally refer to some of these studies to illustrate various points. Our primary reference, however, will be the biblical texts themselves. While this is not a study of biblical eschatology or an explication of biblical prophecy, both of these will of necessity enter the picture from time to time. Primarily, though, this book is about *how* to interpret biblical prophecy. Hence, the focus is on guidelines and principles which will enable the reader to enter with some confidence the world of beasts and dragons, visions and symbols—the world of biblical prophecy.

3
Problems in Interpreting Biblical Prophecy

"**Most important** among the prophecies fulfilled in our time is the rebirth of Israel as a nation. The Bible tells us that in the last days Israel will again become a nation, shortly before the return of Christ. In fact, based on the date of Israel's re-formation, we are able to determine with close approximation the time of the rapture."

It was a weekend conference on biblical prophecy in a nearby church. Scores of people had crowded into the small sanctuary to hear the prophets interpreted, to see the future unveiled. As the keynote speaker promised to date the rapture, ears perked up and people slid forward in their seats, hungry with anticipation. The speaker continued.

"The Bible says that Jesus will return within one generation after the rebirth of Israel as a nation. We have determined a 'generation' in the Bible to be forty years. So watch carefully as we apply biblical mathematics.

"First, Israel was restored as a nation in 1948 in the after-

math of World War 2." Here his marker streaked across the
overhead projector, displaying the all-important date.

"Now if we add one generation to 1948 . . . that's 1948 plus
40 equals . . . 1988. So the second coming of Christ is dated in
1988." More figuring on the overhead projector.

"But remember, we have seen earlier this weekend that
seven years before Jesus' return the church, the true church,
will be taken up in the rapture, before the time of the tribulation. Therefore, we subtract seven years from 1988 . . .

"So we can be confident that the Scriptures teach that the
rapture will be sometime in 1981. Mark your calendars—
1981."

In dozens of such weekends, in as many churches, this
teacher and others like him proclaimed this message—
through the 1970s and into the decade of the '80s.[1] Of course,
with the dawning of New Year's Day, 1982, this exposition of
the prophetic message fell out of vogue.

In later chapters we will look at some of the assumptions
behind this brand of biblical interpretation and its faithfulness to the prophetic Scriptures. For the present, this story
illustrates well that the way of interpreting prophecy is fraught
with obstacles. Not without good reason are there significant
differences of opinion on these matters—even among those
who share similar views of the inspiration of Scripture. These
difficulties are not insurmountable, however, and need not
sidetrack the would-be interpreter. While it is true that the
words of the prophets may not always be as easily compre-
hended as certain other parts of the Bible, the prophetic message is not therefore completely out of reach. However, if we
want to understand it, we must prayerfully apply care and
diligence to the interpretive task before us.

As we study biblical prophecy, we must be alert to potential
problems. Some of these we can recognize and avoid at the
outset. Others we must simply accept as intrinsic to the task of
handling communications from ancient men of God. These

hurdles fall into two broad categories. On the one hand are those related to our own expectations of the prophets and their words. On the other hand are those inherent in the prophetic Scriptures themselves.

Problems We Bring to the Prophetic Scriptures

Not all difficulties in interpreting prophecy come directly from the Scriptures themselves. Some come from the way we handle them.

Problem 1: Failure to read the text on its own terms. Topping the list of problems is the main difficulty with communication in general and the written word in particular: the ever-present temptation to hear what we want to hear, to see what we want to see. Some people are so much in love that they can find kindling for their inner fire in the most innocent "hello"—as long as it is from that special person. Similarly, some people can prove almost anything with a verse of Scripture. Such practice might take the form of isolating a particular verse or phrase from its context. Or the error may lie in reading modern ideas back into ancient texts. Reading of this sort fails to come to terms with what the author wanted to communicate, what the author intended with those words. The focus shifts, instead, to what we want the author to say. The question of the hour becomes "What does it mean to me?" Rather than molding ourselves to God's Word, we try to remake the Bible in our own image. Not only is this unacceptable biblical interpretation, it is not even good reading technique.[2]

In seeking to understand prophecy, the Christian must first come to grips with what the writer intended in the original context. That is, understanding the author's intended message must precede the further, if equally important, task of applying that message to our own lives. Of course, totally objective reading is impossible. As interpreters we are incapable of completely sundering ourselves from our own limited perspectives. All traces of cultural conditioning cannot be wiped away, nor can all existential concerns and values be swept under the carpet. However, this does not negate the goal of understanding the author's purpose, and biblical interpreters are compelled to pursue it.

Problem 2: Concern with extrabiblical questions. For teaching concerning the rapture, 1 Thessalonians 4:16-17 is pivotal. This passage contains the sole biblical reference to a rapture of believers in association with Jesus' return.[3] Consequently, some persons have approached the text with a mind to procure data for speculation on the end times. But Paul did not write 1 Thessalonians 4:16-17 in order to teach about the rapture or in any way to outline his eschatology. On the contrary, Paul's writing was motivated by an apparent question concerning the fate of the faithful dead.

If, as the Thessalonians had been taught to believe, all believers would see the return of Jesus—that is, the *parousia*—then why had some Christians died prior to the parousia? Verses 13-18 constitute Paul's answer to this concern. Christ's death and resurrection revolutionize how one views death: death is no longer hopelessness. At Jesus' return, the faithful dead will rise first. So, far from missing his return, the dead in Christ will have a prominent place in it. With this line of thought Paul comforts the believers at Thessalonica.

Not end-time speculation, not a systematic eschatology, but the need for comfort among concerned believers provided the impetus for this brief section of Scripture. In light of what will happen, reasons Paul, Christians can have present comfort and hope. Thus, if we take 1 Thessalonians 4:16-17 as a handbook for hypothesizing about the future, we concern ourselves with questions which are foreign to Paul's intent.

The history of Christianity reveals numerous examples of extrabiblical speculation about the end, demonstrating again and again that the Bible is not nearly as interested in tying things down as we have been. Not only have some persons appealed directly to this or that text to gain answers to questions alien to those of the biblical writers, as in the preceding example. In addition, there have been a host of attempts to chart out the future according to the Bible, numerous declarations of the nearness of the end and many bids to apply scriptural arithmetic in order to date Jesus' return.[4]

As early as the second century A.D. a new emphasis on prophetism arose, particularly evident in the Montanist movement. Montanus, a Christian from Phrygia in Asia Minor, led the new movement, having proclaimed himself the mouthpiece of the Spirit. Montanists had a strong faith in the Holy Spirit as the promised Comforter, a belief in the continuance of miraculous gifts, an exacting standard of morality and an eager expectation of Jesus' imminent return. They proclaimed the nearness of the end of the world and the appearance of the New Jerusalem, which would find its place in Phrygia. Because the end was so near, some Montanists were indifferent to the ordinary affairs of this world.[5] However, Montanism, as a formal movement, gradually became extinct without seeing its expectations fulfilled.

As the second century gave way to the third, a decree was issued by the Roman soldier-emperor Severus forbidding people to convert to Christianity or Judaism. At the same time various parts of the empire saw the rise of Christian persecution. In Egypt Christians came under such intense attack that some thought the persecution was a sign of the coming of the last antichrist, the prelude to the last day.[6] But it was not so.

Already in the second century many Christians believed that Jesus' return would follow the first thousand years after his death and resurrection. And, as if to affirm that belief, the religious climate of the years marking the turn of the eleventh century seemed ripe for a sudden climactic event, the Second Coming of Christ. But the end was not yet.

Mathematicians know John Napier as the inventor of logarithms. He also penned a commentary on the book of Revelation which incorporated the time of Jesus' Second Coming. By means of his mathematical prowess Napier calculated Jesus' return to be between 1688 and 1700. Stephen Travis reports that Napier's tome went through twenty-three editions and several translations until 1700. After that, Napier's interpretation was not very convincing.[7]

In the modern era numerous end-time speculations have revolved around World Wars 1 and 2—and now, with some futurists pointing to World War 3, such speculation is undergoing a keen revival. A popular writer tells us that one thing is obvious: "We are moving at an ever-accelerating rate of speed into a prophetic countdown."[8] Even non-Christians viewing the current world situation have introduced into modern vernacular the concept of apocalyptic—used in a secular sense to denote the hopelessness of our future, the inevitability and nearness of our own self-destruction.

So, in regard to end-time theorizing, the modern era is no different from earlier periods. The drive to systematize and chart out the course of history, and especially its ending days, continues to yield fascinating results and impressive time lines. Be that as it may, the fact still stands that the biblical writers had no such pressing concerns. The Bible simply leaves open many questions about the end. The Christian hope—that God will consummate history, fulfill his purpose and bring salvation to his people—is solidly based in the Scriptures. But seeking an exact schedule by which all this happens is an extrabiblical pursuit.

Problems Inherent in the Prophetic Scriptures

In addition to our problems—our mistaken approaches to the biblical texts—a few biblical problems confront interpreters of biblical prophecy. These complexities are associated with the texts themselves.

Problem 3: How literal is the text? In some circles it is proclaimed, at times with great gusto, that every prophecy spoken in the Bible expects a literal fulfillment. Consider, for example, these words of M. R. DeHaan:

Every single prophesied event fulfilled in the past has been literally fulfilled without fail just exactly as the Bible said it would be. Since all fulfilled prophecies have been absolutely reliable, we can with confidence accept all the remaining prophecies of the future with equal certainty. The fulfilled prophecies were brought to pass *literally,* and therefore the unfulfilled prophecies will be consummated with the same literalness.[9]

DeHaan's statement has two points of reference—the one a matter of faith, the other a point of interpretation. His attempt to demonstrate the reliability of those prophecies which have yet to be fulfilled by reference to past fulfillment is at best *a priori.* One might better appeal directly to the utter faithfulness of God, inherent in his character—or to the indwelling presence of the Holy Spirit, given as a deposit guaranteeing the final redemption of God's people (Eph 1:13-14). In point of fact, Christian faith entails risk (Heb 11:1; see also Rom 4:18), and that risk extends to the eschatological future.[10] The truth of predictions cannot be judged before their fulfillment; hence, DeHaan's argument proves nothing.

There is a further, perhaps even more basic, problem present here. It is simply not true that "every single prophesied event fulfilled in the past has been literally fulfilled." Nor is it true that all biblical prophecies expect a literal fulfillment. For example, in his Pentecost address (Acts 2) Peter declares that the prophecy of Joel 2:28-32 was fulfilled at Pentecost. The prophecy is not literally fulfilled, however, for where is the blood, the smoke, the darkened sun, the moon turned to blood? Again, Micah 5:2 predicts that a ruler will come from Bethlehem to reign over Israel. To expect a literal interpretation of this text in Jesus rules out the salvation of non-Israelites. Happily, this prophecy has not been fulfilled in a literalistic manner!

There are three important reasons for not demanding

from biblical prophecy a literal interpretation. The first is that, as is characteristic of the literary forms in which prophecy is given, the language used is often figurative and symbolic, sometimes even fantastic. So, when Isaiah proclaims, "In days to come Jacob will take root, Israel will bud and blossom and fill all the world with fruit" (27:6), we need not expect that Isaiah had in mind a literal (botanical) fulfillment. Nor should we look for a literal beast like a lion with eagle's wings (Dan 7:4). Numbers, too, are often used in a symbolic fashion.

Second, biblical prophecy includes teaching as well as prediction. Some interpreters—for example, Tim LaHaye—give the impression that prophecy is strictly the foretelling of future events.[11] From their writings, one could easily conclude that the biblical prophets were primarily concerned with predicting events in the distant future. Such an understanding, however, is far from the truth. Douglas Stuart, Old Testament scholar at Gordon-Conwell Theological Seminary, writes, "Less than 2 percent of Old Testament prophecy is messianic. Less that 5 percent specifically describes the New Covenant age. Less than 1 percent concerns events yet to come."[12] In point of fact, as we will see, prophecy is *both* prediction and pedagogy—and failure to recognize prophecy's dual character puts the interpreter off the track at the outset.

Third, some prophecies are apparently fulfilled more than once. The example often quoted of this phenomenon is Isaiah 7:14: "Therefore the Lord himself will give you a sign: The virgin will be with child and will give birth to a son, and will call him Immanuel." According to the context of the passage in Isaiah, the promised child was to be God's sign to King Ahaz in the days of Ahaz and Isaiah. Matthew, however, quotes this prophecy and proclaims its fulfillment in the birth of Jesus (1:23). Indeed, it is often the case that the New Testament finds in the Old surprising nuances, a point to which we will turn in some detail later.

Problem 4: Contextual complexities. The writings that we call biblical prophecy present a variety of literary forms. In addition to the broad designations of *prophetic* and *apocalyptic* which we will discuss below, we also find prophetic oracles, laments, symbolic actions, visions, prayers, poetry, sayings and narrative. In interpreting a prophetic passage, we have to consider each literary form it may contain. This complexity is most readily seen in the book of Revelation since its literary form, or genre, is a matter of some debate. Is it to be interpreted against a prophetic backdrop or within an apocalyptic matrix? What are we to make of its form as an epistle? How did John intend the book to be read? With what literary form did he intend to identify the Revelation?

Likewise, locating a conceptual background for the book is difficult. The book of Revelation is saturated with allusions to the Old Testament. It draws on Daniel and Ezekiel as well as, to a lesser degree, Zechariah, Isaiah, Joel and others. In his *New Testament Introduction,* Donald Guthrie reports that of Revelation's 404 verses only 126 contain no allusion to the Old Testament.[13] Besides the Old Testament, John seems to have drawn images from noncanonical Jewish apocalyptic and even from ancient mythology. Further, early Christian worship appears to be reflected in Revelation in the form of hymnody and liturgy quoted or adapted in the book.

When confronted with such complexities, students of Revelation may feel overwhelmed! Surely, they may think, an extensive background in Judaism, Hellenism, early Christianity and Latin history must be prerequisite to unlocking its message. To be sure, background knowledge of this sort can be helpful to the interpreter. Nevertheless, the message of John's Revelation is not the sole possession of the academics. Throughout the history of the church, particularly in times of persecution and despair, Revelation has spoken a powerful word of hope even to unlearned Christians.

Problem 5: Historical distance. A person who has taken notes at a lecture or seminar may know the experience of later returning to those notes and wondering, "Now, what was that all about?" Separated by the lapse of even a few days, what once seemed crystal clear becomes dark and shadowy. How much more difficulty we encounter in reading age-old texts which, to our misfortune, do not always give indications of setting, purpose and audience!

Images and means of expression fall out of vogue with the passing of time. Imagine our progeny of two or three thousand years hence coming across political cartoons of our day—complete with donkeys and elephants, or a report of a "bullish" stock market! An even more basic problem than interpreting symbols, though, is trying to contextualize the prophetic messages now that many particulars of Israel's national life are lost to us.

Problem 6: Analyzing the future. It is one thing to take a test tube of an unknown substance into the laboratory for the purpose of determining its make-up. Tests can be run and rerun. Laboratory procedures can be checked and rechecked. Certainty can be reached. It is quite another thing to fit matters of eschatology under the microscope, for then one attempts to gaze at what cannot be seen, to analyze what has not yet happened. Empirical substantiation cannot be called into play. Furthermore, such eschatological concepts as the resurrection of the dead and even the Second Coming of Jesus are matters of faith and are not in themselves subject to scientific inquiry. Certainty, then, is difficult to achieve.

In this chapter we have only set the agenda for what is to come. Enough has been said, however, to indicate why many of the so-called experts on prophecy disagree, even sharply. And enough has been said to indicate the earnestness which must characterize our endeavor to understand the message of the prophets.

4
Prophecy
as
Scripture

I know you believe you know what I said. But I am not sure *you realize that what you heard is not what I meant.* This clever adage found on wall posters indicates the difficulties associated with so natural, and apparently so simple, a thing as talking. In reality, hurdles to good communication abound! Sometimes other noises—like that of radios and televisions—obstruct our hearing. Sometimes our diction is slurred. Sometimes our thoughts are muddled. Sometimes we use figures of speech or draw on experiences unfamiliar to our listeners. And sometimes we use words and phrases whose meanings change with time and locale. In the context of such obstacles, communication is carried on—or attempted—daily.

Many stumbling blocks associated with verbal communication are also found in the written word. One has only to pick up a copy of Einstein's *Theory of Relativity,* an early edition of Dante's *Inferno* or Rudolf Bultmann's *Kerygma and Myth* to experience this truth. The problems are only magnified when we turn to literature written in alien cultures and unknown languages.

Whatever else it is, the Bible is a book which seeks to communicate by means of words and phrases, sentences and paragraphs. So it, like any other book, is not without its interpretive perplexities. This is true for the Bible as a whole, and particularly for biblical prophecy. The first step in marshalling principles for understanding prophecy is to get a good handle on the essentials of biblical interpretation, and that is the subject of this chapter.[1]

A Divine and Human Word

At least at the outset, the Bible is subject to the same rules of interpretation as other literary works. However, we cannot stop with this conclusion, since a myriad of literary forms exists, each with its own principles of interpretation. For example, we would not unlock the meaning of a poetic work with the same key that we might use in studying a historical biography. Similarly, the telephone book gives different information from a chemistry textbook. A single author might pen books so varied as to require different approaches for proper understanding—compare C. S. Lewis's children's fantasy *Chronicles of Narnia* with his theological treatise *The Problem of Pain*. To comprehend the message of an author, then, we must ask what the writer intended to convey with this more or less orderly aggregate of words. What sort of writing is this, and what was the motivation behind its being written? With regard to the Bible the questions remain the same. What, then, are the answers?

Evident already is the Bible's affinity with other kinds of written communication. Like them, it is the fruit of human hands, produced in the crucible of human experience. In its pages we find human emotions, human relationships, human history and human needs—all from a human perspective. Yet the Bible is not merely a human statement, and so it must be set apart from other literary works.[2] Though certainly written by human hands in the language and thought-patterns of real people from other ages and cultures, the Bible is more: it is a word from God. Among all the volumes ever written, the Bible is unique in its character as both a human and a divine word.

To assert the Bible is God's word is not to render it untouchable, as if it belonged locked away or on display in a glass case. Yet too often the Bible is treated just so, hidden among the "family treasures" or occupying its special place on the coffee table or bureau. Nor would we extend to the Bible a magical quality, to be used the same way as a rabbit's foot or lucky charm.

Again, to claim the Bible is God's word is never to argue that God could not, or does not, operate through other means to reveal truth. God may speak to us through many avenues—through creation, a wise (or not so wise) friend, a book, a vision or even a sermon. After all, Numbers 22 tells how God communicated his message with the help of a donkey! Here we are simply recognizing that in the Bible God speaks to us in a unique way. Consequently, the Bible is not to be sneered at or shrugged off, like some astrological column or biorhythmic chart, or last week's best-selling novel. It is important for us to recognize the Bible's character as a divine and human word as we try to understand its message.

The affirmation, "the Bible is God's word," is a two-pronged declaration. First, the Bible is God's word within a particular historical setting. That is, God chose to express himself in particular ways to particular people at particular times. Hence, each biblical text is a product of certain, now past, circumstances. Each book is shaped by the culture, thought-patterns and language of its own day. Second, because the Bible is God's word, God continues to reveal himself through it. That is, the biblical texts have relevance beyond their original historical peculiarities.

Understanding these distinctions is vital to interpreting the

Scriptures correctly. To deny the first is to render the Bible little more than a legal code or an arsenal from which to launch proof texts for the latest pet concern. Those who neglect the historical aspect of God's Word assert, in effect, "Tell me what you want the Bible to say and I will find you a verse to prove it." There are, for example, those who assert emphatically that bringing Christmas trees into the house is sin, on the basis of such texts as Isaiah 57:5, "You burn with lust among the oaks and under every spreading tree"; who outline a doctrine of separation of Whites from Blacks, based on Acts 17:26, "From one man [God] made every nation . . . and he determined . . . the exact places where they should live"; who teach a new prosperity for all Christians—no more sickness, no more financial problems—based on texts like Philippians 4:19, "And my God will meet all your needs."

Others have equated baptism and salvation (Mk 16:16), advocated snake handling as an element of worship (Mk 16:18) and practiced baptism for the dead (1 Cor 15:29)—all as a result of neglecting the original historical reference of the given biblical texts.[3] Biblical interpretation thus becomes an exercise in subjectivism: this text means whatever I want it to mean.

On the other hand, failure to recognize the eternal relevance of the Bible renders it a mere book of the past. Thus, as a piece of literature—or, rather, as a collection of literary works—the Bible is an interesting object for inquiry and research. It tells us what certain people of old thought about God, and it may even be viewed as source material for piecing together aspects of ancient history. But the Bible has nothing to say to us today, no claim on our lives. It is simply a large set of pages from history which, luckily, survived into modernity.

Viewing the Bible as God's word to a particular historical setting while retaining its quality as God's continuing self-revelation avoids these two interpretive flaws. In its original setting the biblical text was both a divine and a human word. So it remains today—and in that lies the key for understanding the Bible's significance for our own lives. The problem is this: our historical situation is not theirs. Nuclear weaponry, birth-control pills, rock music and the modern cinema simply are not *specifically* mentioned in age-old writings. Nevertheless, because God chose to reveal himself in the course of real human history in Scripture, we may take courage that these same words can speak again in other situations, including our own.[4]

How does this happen? The cardinal rule for applying Scripture to our situation is easily asserted: The significance of a passage for us must flow from its meaning in its own context. Hence, biblical interpretation is essentially a two-step process. First, we view the Bible against its own background. Second, we translate the biblical message into our own life-setting. How to accomplish these two steps will come in for further explication shortly. Before that, however, a brief look at "literal interpretation" is in order.

The Problems with Literalism

Should the Bible always be understood literally? Happily, we have not seen much confusion about whether or not to literally understand Jesus' words in Matthew 5:29—"If your right eye causes you to sin, gouge it out and throw it away." In the area of biblical prophecy the issue takes on great significance. One need not read very far in the ever-growing literature on biblical prophecy to discern the import given to "literal" versus "nonliteral" methods. For example, as one gets further and further into Hal Lindsey's popular paperback *The Late Great Planet Earth,* one grows weary of his repetitive emphasis on "literalism." For Lindsey, though, the matter cannot be asserted too emphatically. He sees the issue as a straight, black-and-white proposition: Either the prophetic Scriptures are interpreted literally, thus rightly—or they are interpreted allegorically, thus wrongly.[5] Agreeing with

Lindsey in emphasis is J. Dwight Pentecost who, in his well-known volume *Things to Come,* even asserts that the method of literal interpretation characterized Jesus' and the early church's uses of Scripture. He contends:

> The original and accepted method of interpretation was the literal method, which was used by the Lord, the greatest interpreter, and any other method was introduced to promote heterodoxy. Therefore, the literal method must be accepted as the basic method for right interpretation in any field of doctrine today.[6]

We will deal with the notion of the literal fulfillment of prophecies elsewhere; here we must look at two more general problems with Pentecost's statement about literal interpretation.

First, there is no simple either-or choice between literal and other forms of interpretation. The history of biblical interpretation reveals many divergent paths, demonstrating the complexities inherent in the task. Indeed, the early Christian theologian best known for his tendencies toward allegorical interpretation, Origen, applied the technique only in his struggle to come to grips with such complexities. The New Testament's use of the Old Testament, or even Jesus' use of the Old Testament, shows that the picture is much more varied than persons like Pentecost would have us think. For instance, Paul intentionally employs allegory in Galatians 4 where he refers to the story of Abraham and his two sons, born to him by the slave woman (Hagar) and the free woman (Sarah).[7] Again, in 1 Corinthians 10:1-13, Paul explicitly uses a typological argument—using the Greek words for "type" *(typos)* and "typologically" *(typikos)* in verses 6 and 11—to introduce his warnings concerning the Lord's Supper. In actuality, New Testament writers, and even Jesus, used a whole range of interpretive methods that were accepted in their day.[8] Thus to insist on an either-or choice is to fail to account for all the evidence.

Lindsey himself is guilty of oversimplifying the problem.

For example, while he insists that we must read the prophetic texts literally, even he is capable of finding in predictions of Christ's return "with the clouds of heaven" references to "myriads of believers who return in white robes with Jesus."[9] He can write concerning John, author of Revelation:

> To his primitive eye, the beasts looked like lions wearing armored breastplates. They spit something like fire from their mouths. I believe this 1st century prophet saw 20th century battle tanks or armored personnel carriers.[10]

Again, Lindsey can, with a fine allegorical brush, outline the character qualities of the beast prophesied in Revelation 13:2.[11] According to the canon Lindsey himself establishes for understanding biblical prophecy, his interpretation falls short. But the problem is not that he has failed to use a literal method. Rather, as Lindsey himself demonstrates, the problem is that not all biblical texts are intended to be interpreted literally. This brings us to the second problem with Pentecost's view of literal interpretation.

We have previously observed that different forms of literature require different rules or principles for proper understanding. That is, a particular piece of writing should be interpreted with regard to the category of literature (or genre) into which it falls. If the author has given us a folktale, we ought to read it as a folktale; if a biography, as a biography; if a poem, as a poem; and so on. This is true for seminars in English literature and for the study of the Bible.

We have already seen how this perspective applies to the whole Bible as a human and divine word; now we must further note its application to each part of the Bible, for the Scriptures are made up of a host of literary forms. The Bible contains proverbs, all sorts of poetry, prophetic utterances, hymns, letters, apocalyptic discourses, sermons and historical narratives, to name only a few of its ingredients. Many errors in interpretation may be "cut off at the pass" simply by recognizing the literary form of each biblical text as it is considered.[12]

Even a Gospel like Mark or Matthew (itself a kind of literature) mixes with the narrative literary form such genres as the parable (for example, Mark 4:1-8) and the apocalyptic discourse (such as Mark 13). About these kinds of differences James W. Sire writes:

> If we recognize that Jesus' story of the sower and the seed is a parable, we will not spend our time looking for the field in Palestine to which Jesus was referring. On the other hand, if we recognize that John was narrating an actual event in John 4, we may be helped by picturing the scene in our mind's eye and recapturing the drama of an actual event in Jesus' life. We may even be able to find the place where the well was located when Jesus spoke to the Samaritan woman.[13]

Because of the diversity of literary forms, then, it is certainly too simplistic to assert a literalistic method as the one guiding rule of interpretation.

So, when DeHaan reports that his discussion of biblical prophecy allows us to fit whatever happens today into its place in God's program, we must ask, Is this the proper way to use the prophetic texts?[14] Similarly, when LaHaye sees in Daniel 12:4 ("many shall run to and fro") a reference to twentieth-century technological advances in the transportation industry, we must wonder if LaHaye has read Daniel in the same spirit in which it was written.[15] Has he a good handle on the message *intended by the text?*

In the next chapter we shall begin discussing an alternative approach to the prophetic (and apocalyptic-prophetic) form of literature. Enough has been said to indicate the difficulties in trying to interpret everything in the Bible literally;[16] in point of fact, the text's literary form and context must determine how it is to be interpreted. With this excursus on biblical literalism behind us, we may now return to the problem of viewing the Bible in its own context, thus to draw from it a message for our own day.

Finding the Text's Original Meaning

The initial task confronting the student of the Scriptures is to uncover the original meaning of the text for its original audience. What circumstances motivated the writing of this passage, this book? Why was it written in this way, with these words? What was the author trying to say to his readers? These questions and others like them help us discover the message of a given biblical text.

We might take, for example, Paul's first letter to the Corinthians. From the letter itself we can begin to see why Paul wrote as he did. Paul addressed this letter to the Christians at Corinth in response to some disturbing reports he had received from Chloe's household (1 Cor 1:11). Additionally, he had received from the Corinthians a letter about certain issues needing his response (see 1 Cor 7:1). We must first read 1 Corinthians in the light of this information, interpreting the letter by attempting to discover what Paul wanted to say to the *Corinthians*—and not yet what he might be saying to *us*.

This process of discovering the original meaning may appear to be a difficult assignment; admittedly, certain texts are fraught with problems. But in the main, and certainly for matters of great significance, good Bible study is not beyond the reach of any believer. The availability of good tools and reference works helps to bring the original meaning even closer. The questions which follow are designed to help you to understand what the Bible means in its own historical context.

1. Which Bible should I use? The Bible was originally written in Hebrew (most of the Old Testament), Greek (New Testament) and Aramaic (parts of Ezra and Daniel). Attempts to render these ancient languages into understandable English have resulted in a smorgasbord of translations from which to choose. It is best to use a combination of good English translations in Bible study. For an accurate translation in easily digested English one can hardly do better than the New International Version (NIV), though some might prefer the New English Bible (NEB), Jerusalem Bible (JB), or Good News Bible (GNB—also known as Today's English Version). In its attempt to present concepts in modern vernacular, the NIV sacrifices some literalism. Hence, a good second translation for study would be a more literal translation, like the New American Standard Bible (NASB), the Revised Standard Version (RSV), or even the King James Version (KJV). Most Bibles published recently are the fruit of many years of hard work by translation committees. This process makes for an accurate translation, but something still may be said in favor of those Bibles translated by individuals—for example, Williams or Phillips. Sometimes referred to as "free translations," these Bibles often use expressions which add color and highlight particular nuances in the biblical text. They can help make the text come alive. A number of additional versions could be mentioned, but the point is this: it is best to study with a representative translation from each category—modern English, literal and free. The Living Bible is not a translation, but a paraphrase, and is unsuitable for serious study.

2. *What is the historical context of this passage?* Having chosen a text for study, we must at the outset determine its historical context. We want information on the social and cultural setting of the text and the people to whom it was addressed, the background of its issues and thought, and other data (such as geographical and political) which provide the frame of reference for the biblical passage. Why are Psalms 120—134 entitled "Songs of Ascents," and what particular historical situation do they all reflect? What is the controversy behind meat sacrificed to idols? How did it arise, and why is the issue mentioned in Acts, Romans, 1 Corinthians and Revelation?

Introductions to the Bible and Bible dictionaries give assistance in this area. For the Old Testament a good reference work is R. K. Harrison's *Introduction to the Old Testament* (Eerdmans); for the New, see *New Testament Introduction* by Donald Guthrie (InterVarsity). *The New Bible Dictionary: Revised* (Tyndale) and *The Zondervan Pictorial Bible Dictionary* (Zondervan) are good one-volume selections. In two volumes is the *Wycliffe Bible Encyclopedia* (Moody)—also an excellent choice.

The author's purpose also falls under this heading of historical context. In "days of old" writing was not simply a matter of picking up the handiest stationery and pen; thus inquiring into the occasion of his writing is no moot exercise. Why did he write at all? What was going on in Israel, or in the church, which might have motivated his work? Why did he express these particular concerns? What goings-on were behind Habakkuk's angry outburst at God? What was happening at Galatia that resulted in Paul's calling the Galatians foolish? These questions and others like them can be answered by consulting the text itself, though we may wish to compare our notes with the comments found in a Bible dictionary or introduction.

3) What is the literary context of this passage? We recognize that in the Bible thoughts are communicated through words, which find their meaning in phrases, sentences and collections of sentences—all in some orderly fashion. But what order? We want to know how the author places this particular sentence in relation to others, how this particular passage is placed in its larger setting and in the book as a whole. Whatever the form of the text (for example, prose or verse), the author must have had some reason for the ordering of his material, some sort of outline. The task at hand is to determine that outline—to determine the argument, the progression of thought inherent in the text itself. How does verse 5 relate to verse 15? How does the second half of the book relate to the first? How has the author developed his point?

It can be readily seen that this discipline rules out the popular practice of ripping a verse from its place in the book. Instead, what comes to the fore is how a verse or group of verses is connected to surrounding verses—how it relates to what goes before and what goes after. This step in the study ought to be pursued without the help of "the experts," though, again, one may wish to consult appropriate commentaries to compare findings.[17] Most commentaries, in fact, begin with an outline of the biblical book.

4. How were the words used when this text was written? Words not only differ in their usage from place to place, but also tend to undergo metamorphosis with time. So words do not always mean what they seem. Moreover, some words are used in a variety of unrelated ways. For example, when you hear the word *can,* what comes to mind? The answer will depend on your frame of reference. *Can* might mean any of a number of things, to as many different people:

☐ Putting up tomatoes for the winter
☐ A prison
☐ File 13
☐ A container
☐ A unit of measure
☐ The toilet
☐ A verb, meaning "to be able to"
☐ The process of making a phonograph record
☐ In old poetry, "began"
☐ What the boss does when firing an employee
☐ A type of dancer—a "Can-Can Girl"
☐ _____

To determine what *I* mean when *I* use the word *can,* a person must consider the context in which *I* use it. Likewise, in the New Testament, confusion over word usage is possible. *World* can be used to describe the object of God's love (Jn 3:16), that which must not be loved (1 Jn 2:15-17), and our present dwelling place (Jn 16:33). In Galatians Paul can use one word, *flesh,* to mean both "body" (2:20) and "sinful nature" (5:16). *Context determines meaning.*

In addition to consulting the context, though that is certainly the most important reference, one can also benefit from using a good English dictionary. (How else will one ever know what debauchery is?)[18] Concordances, such as *Cruden's Complete Concordance, The NIV Complete Concordance, Strong's Exhaustive Concordance* or *Young's Analytical Concordance,* are helpful in tracing how a word is used in a particular book or by a certain author.

Of course, it is not enough to do the background work; we must go on to state as concisely as possible what the author was trying to communicate to his own readers. Having arrived at this point, we are ready to move on to the second part of the interpretive process—translating the biblical message into our own life-setting.

Applying the Text to Our Lives

For the Christian, Bible study is no mere academic exercise. The believer goes to the Bible to gain more than general Bible knowledge, or to impress someone by quoting scriptural texts or to perform well on a Bible quiz. The Christian views the Scriptures as a word from God and studies it accordingly. In studying them he or she asks: What is God saying to me? To my family? To my church? To my society? To my world? The believer studies in order to know God and his ways more fully —and the difference such knowledge could and should be making in the modern situation. Hence, the temptation is always present to forgo the first step of biblical study, the historical inquiry, and move directly into "what the Bible says to me." That whisper in the ear encourages us to treat the biblical text as a jumping-off place or as an authority to be cited to undergird what we wanted to say all along. And why not?— after all, we have already indicated that the Bible is not strictly timebound; it is ever relevant.

The reason we must take step one before step two is that here lies the only control for rightly understanding what the Bible has to say. The message in its historical context never

changes. It is concrete and objective. It is the constant in the
formula of biblical interpretation. It is from this historical
message that the message for today must flow. The "meaning for us" of this message, its application to our own life-
setting, is not constant. As our circumstances change, the way
the biblical text confronts us will change. But the original
meaning of the text never changes. And, unless we have ac-
cess to that original meaning, nothing will keep us on track
with our interpretation of the Bible. Biblical interpretation
would then become an exercise in subjectivism.

The message of the Bible for today flows from its meaning
in its own historical context. Step one precedes and leads to
step two.

The problem, of course, is that the Scriptures deal with
some problems we do not have, and do not deal with some
problems we have. For example, circumcision was a big issue
in the early church, but faith nowadays hardly rests on that
question. Others in biblical times were concerned with temple
prostitutes; hopefully that problem has not recently come before the board of your church! The military draft, masturba-
tion, television, genetic engineering—these issues confront
some contemporary Christians, but one would be hard-
pressed to find these words listed in a Bible concordance. The
Bible simply does not speak to certain issues in a direct way.
What are Christians to do? Are we to conclude that the Bible
has no guidance to offer? Are we to be our own master and
chart our own course through these problems of today? While
we cannot here go into any great detail in addressing this problem, we can mention two brief points.[19]

First, on some specifics the Bible speaks very clearly to the
modern era, where our circumstances and theirs are not in-
compatible. Once one understands the historical meaning of
certain biblical passages, the same message can be directly applied to the modern era. It is still true, as it was when Paul
wrote to the Romans, that all are under sin (Rom 1:18—3:20).

While some of the words may need to be updated, much of the Sermon on the Mount (Mt 5—7) has direct application to our own day, as do many of the ethical imperatives of the New Testament letters (such as Eph 4:31-32).

When our circumstances do not coincide with those of the biblical setting, our aim must be to sense from our study of the writer's meaning how he would express this message were he writing today. What principle is the biblical writer explicating? How does that principle relate to the modern situation? So, although the Bible does not list the television shows we should or should not watch or prescribe how much time we should spend viewing television, it does have much to say about slavery to things, about using time wisely and about our value systems. While Paul's words in Galatians 5:2 ("Mark my words! I, Paul, tell you that if you let yourselves be circumcised, Christ will be of no value to you at all") may at first sight appear irrelevant to us, we must nevertheless note this warning against setting up any human work as prerequisite to salvation.

The procedure suggested by these examples follows three steps. First, be able to recognize a biblical message which has no direct application to the contemporary situation. Second, seek after the principle embodied in the message, its underlying intention. Third, ask how this principle can be fleshed out in your own life-situations.

These suggestions for biblical application are primarily concerned with how we live as Christians. In other matters to which the Bible speaks, such as points of doctrine, we should always remember that here also the Bible provides the criterion for its own interpretation. Scripture cannot be disregarded simply because we find it objectionable on this or that point.

Passage of time and changes in culture introduce certain difficulties for any who would understand and apply the message of the Bible. But the Bible does have a message for our generation, and that message is a word from God. Christians everywhere are invited, even called, to seriously inquire into what the Scriptures meant long ago and what they mean today.

5
Prophecy
as
Genre

"The Law and the Prophets" is a common characterization of the Old Testament. While this description does not adequately account for the rich literary diversity of the Jewish Scriptures, it does indicate for us the significant niche filled by the prophets throughout Old Testament history. As God's mouthpiece, Moses was first given the title *prophet* (Num 12: 6-8; Deut 34:10), and with him the prophetic line was initiated (Deut 18:14-16).[1] Around the tenth and into the ninth centuries B.C., prophecy began to make its voice heard in such persons as Samuel and Nathan, Elijah and Elisha. Elijah was considered a prominent figure for centuries (Mal 4:5; Mk 8:28; 15:35-36), but "biblical prophecy" usually calls to mind the classical prophets. To this family belongs the succession of prophets from the eighth century forward—Amos, Isaiah, Ezekiel, Joel, Malachi and so on. Present already among the classical prophets in seedling form, apocalyptic—a new thought pattern and literary phenomenon—began to blossom in the centuries just before Jesus' birth. Then, after a long period of silence, the prophetic "word of the Lord" was again heard—in John the Baptist, Jesus and Christian prophecy.[2]

Our special interest lies in the Old Testament with the classical prophets and in the New Testament with Jesus and John, the author of Revelation. Our interest is not merely academic; rather, we want to grasp the prophets' message and see its relevance for our own day. Of course, as we have seen, our initial step is to understand what the prophets were saying in their own days to their contemporaries. What can we learn about the character of prophecy and its close kin, apocalyptic, that will point us on the right interpretive path? What information about the prophets' backgrounds will assist us in understanding their message? And what landmarks should we look for as we survey the terrain offered by God's prophets? These are the kinds of questions facing us in this chapter as we explore the background and character of prophecy. Our agenda begins with Deuteronomy 18:14-22, which provides a paradigm for God's prophet. We continue with a sketch of the prophetic tradition, and its apocalyptic counterpart, through John's Revelation.

Israel's Prophetic Distinctiveness

Set in the midst of an extended address by Moses on the law, Deuteronomy 18:14-22 speaks particularly to the means by which Israel will know the word of the Lord. Already in 18: 9-13 Israel has been warned against submitting to the influence of its neighbor-nations. Foreign practices—child sacrifices, spell casting, consulting the dead, to name a few—were detestable to the Lord. They were the basis for God's judgment on the Canaanites. According to the covenant established between the Lord and his people, he would provide the land and the associated blessings, and they would keep faith, remaining blameless before the Lord. Israel's distinctiveness in religious practice is then extended to the area of prophecy. "The nations" had their own "prophets," their own means of soliciting a divine communiqué—sorcery, divina-

tion, witchcraft and spiritism. But Israel was to have nothing
to do with these mantic and occult practices.[3] Among the
peoples, Israel would be set apart, and so would its prophetic
tradition.

A number of peculiarities spell out the uniqueness of
Israel's prophets. The first, and most basic, is found in the
assertion: "The Lord your God will raise up for you a prophet
like me from among your own brothers" (Deut 18:15). Characteristic of Israel's prophets is their divine call. Not on the
basis of any hereditary right, qualifying position or previous
experience, but only on the basis of a direct call from God
himself were persons appointed prophets. Amos illustrates
this point in his brief recounting of his call:

> I was neither a prophet nor a prophet's son, but I was a
> shepherd, and I also took care of sycamore-fig trees. But
> the LORD took me from tending the flock and said to me,
> "Go, prophesy to my people Israel." (Amos 7:14-15)

As credentials, all Amos can offer is his commissioning by
God. But that is all any prophet can offer!

As for Moses, we may read of his call from God in Exodus 3
and 4. Even as Moses is the *original model* prototype of Israel's prophets,
his encounter with God sets the pattern, if only broadly, for
the divine call. First comes the theophany, or appearance of
God, in which God identifies himself to Moses (Ex 3:1-6).
Then follows the announcement of Moses' having been
chosen to serve as God's instrument (3:7-10). The process continues with Moses' objections and declarations of unworthiness, answered by God's assurance, promise and sign (3:11—
4:17).

Certain parallels to this story in content, if not in order, are
seen in the celebrated account of Isaiah's call. A vision of the
Lord (Is 6:1-4) is followed by Isaiah's realization and confession of his sin, his unworthiness before the Lord (6:5). After-
ward Isaiah's unclean lips are made pure, his guilt taken away,
his sin forgiven (6:6-7). Finally Isaiah receives and answers

his commission to "go and tell the people" (6:8-13). The story of Jeremiah's call (Jer 1:4-8) underscores these same features. What we find, then, is that persons become prophets through God's initiative. God chooses whomever he will, calling those who are ill-prepared and unworthy (sinners, that is), and by an act of grace appoints them as bearers of his word.

Of course, once called, the prophet is not left to his or her own devices, as Deuteronomy 18:18 demonstrates: "I will put my words in his mouth, and he will tell them everything I command him." The prophet is the divine mouthpiece, the authorized spokesperson for God. Thus the capstone to the calling of Jeremiah is the certainty that he has been given the word of the Lord. "Then the LORD reached out his hand and touched my mouth and said to me, 'Now, I have put my words in your mouth' " (Jer 1:9).

The longer narrative in Ezekiel 3 graphically illustrates this same point, symbolized in Ezekiel's actions. He is told to go and speak, but only after having eaten the scroll (words of lament, mourning and woe—2:9-10) given him by the Lord. Israel's prophets were set apart, not to propagate "the delusions of their minds" (Jer 23:26), but to proclaim the word of the Lord. The prophetic vocation was most often carried out in the form of an oracle—the prophet spoke the Lord's message in the first person, usually with the introductory expression "Thus says the Lord" or "This is the word of the Lord."

Called of God and bearing God's word, the prophet of Israel has divine authority. Hence, "you must listen to him" (Deut 18:15). Those who fail to take seriously the prophet's words are answerable to God himself (Deut 18:19). As God's representatives Israel's prophets speak with God's authority. This authority is not, however, inherent in the prophet himself; it rests in the One who called the prophet. The prophet mediates the word by which the Lord reveals and accomplishes his purposes.[4] And that word must not be taken lightly—it is active and powerful. In the words of Isaiah 55:10-11,

As the rain and the snow come down from heaven, and do not return to it without watering the earth and making it bud and flourish, so that it yields seed for the sower and bread for the eater, so is my word that goes out from my mouth: it will not return to me empty, but will accomplish what I desire and achieve the purpose for which I sent it.

Because the authentic word of the Lord "accomplishes itself," as it were, true prophecy can be distinguished from false. "If what a prophet proclaims in the name of the LORD does not take place or come true, that is a message the LORD has not spoken" (Deut 18:22). Actually, Moses here appears to be drawing up not one, but two criteria for distinguishing the Lord's message. The more obvious is found in the first clause: "if it does not take place." At this point we are concerned with judgmental or predictive prophecy—the truth of the words rests in their fulfillment. This form of validation is likewise set forth by Jeremiah (28:9) for those who prophesy peace.

The second criterion is more difficult to grasp in the translation above, since "take place" and "come true" seem synonymous. More literally one might read, "the word is not," or, then, "if what the prophet says is not so." "That is, the word supposedly spoken by God through the prophet was not in accord with the word of God already revealed and it was therefore automatically suspect."[5] These two tests were to be applied to any prophecies spoken in the name of the Lord. Verse 20 has already declared invalid and worthy of the most severe judgment any who prophesy in the name of other gods. Similarly, anyone who entices Israel to follow other gods, or who in any way tries to turn others away from the Lord God, is a false prophet to be stoned to death (Deut 13).

Before departing from Deuteronomy 18, we must give attention to one further point—the far-reaching vision of this passage on prophets. We have previously indicated that Moses, the prototype of the prophet of Israel, was first in a long line of true prophets of the Lord. In the qualities we have outlined, Israel's prophets would be "like Moses." In time, however, the "prophet like me" about whom Moses spoke took on a fuller, eschatological significance. That is, many came to believe that Moses' words had a future point of reference, that in the last days God would raise up a great prophetic mediator.[6] Consistent with this Jewish expectation, and perhaps taking its cue from Jesus' own prophetic self-understanding (see Mark 6:4; Luke 13:31-33), early Christians identified the "prophet like Moses" with Jesus (Acts 3: 17-23). Indeed, the parallels between Moses and Jesus are striking: Moses mediated God's covenant with Israel and was instrumental in establishing the kingdom of Israel; Jesus mediated the "new covenant" (Lk 22:20) and instituted the kingdom of God. Thus Moses' statement about prophecy was regarded as an indicator of things to come.

The Historical Backdrop

Centuries after Moses, the first of the Old Testament prophetic books were written. The great epoch of prophecy began with Amos and Hosea, both from the mid-eighth century B.C. Viewed against the totality of Israel's history, this era, dating from approximately 760 into the mid 400s B.C., covers a rather restricted time span. That it was an important time, important to Israel's faith, is evident from the concentration of prophetic writings from this period in the Old Testament.

In order to grasp the significance of the prophetic activity of this epoch, as well as to understand the prophets' message, one must become familiar with that age. To a substantial degree the prophets spoke directly to events in their world; even prophetic pointers to future happenings served as warning or encouragement for the prophets' contemporaries. A careful reading of the historical narratives, 1—2 Kings and 1—2 Chronicles, sets the stage for understanding this prophetic period. Specifics regarding the frame of reference in which each of the prophets delivered their respective messages may be gained from Bible introductions and dictionaries, or from individual commentaries. Here we can paint the picture with only the broadest of strokes.[7]

Toward the end of the tenth century B.C., Solomon died, leaving as his legacy an oppressive administrative policy which had alienated northern Israel. Solomon's son, Rehoboam, chose to perpetuate that policy (1 Kings 12:1-15), to the end that the kingdom of Israel was divided. The empire gave way to two states—Israel in the north, Judah in the south. Economically and socially, the two realms came under immediate stress, the result of inner struggles and sporadic sectional warfare following the schism. Though in later years they were to experience economic revival, the coming days were fraught with other, more far-reaching disasters.

Israel, in the north, encountered tension from all sides. Politically, extreme internal instability resulted from the violent removal of three kings in just over four decades (1 Kings 15:25—16:23). In addition, outside threat came, most significantly, from Assyria, an old world power reborn, which was flexing its mighty military muscles at the expense of neighboring nations. Economically, there was eventual good news —but the material prosperity was hardly spread evenly, and the condition of the peasantry deteriorated. Class distinctions —the rich versus the poor—arose.

Such disarray inevitably pointed to problems in the national religion, for in the days of ancient Israel religious life covered all other areas—national life, social life, economics. Religion and culture were indistinguishable; indeed, such categorization of life and experience is a relatively modern invention. In fact, the religious life of the northern state was rotting, a cancerous infection reaching to all its vital organs.

From the beginning, the new state of Israel had provided its own shrines for worship, thus seeking to fill the void from the loss of Jerusalem (now capital of Judah) as worship center. These new shrines and accompanying religious practices, *departure from one's religion.*

however, opened the way for mass idolatry (1 Kings 12:25-33). The flames of apostasy were vigorously fanned by Jezebel, foreign wife of King Ahab, who apparently sought to make the cult of Baal the official religion of the court. Although the worship of Yahweh, the Lord, continued to enjoy official status, by the eighth century the Mosaic covenant was all but forgotten. Local houses of worship had been paganized, and the worship of Baal was widespread. An inner perversion of Israel's faith had taken place. Such developments found no rebuke from complacent priests and prophetic orders who turned a blind eye to the adulteration of Israel's faith. The centerpiece of that faith, the covenant, was lost in religious ritual.

In the south, Judah had problems parallel to those in Israel, though on a reduced scale. Importantly, Judah enjoyed greater internal stability than did its northern neighbor. "Judah did evil in the eyes of the LORD" (1 Kings 14:22), but its record of disobedience to the covenant did not compare with that of Israel. Nevertheless, religious tolerance and paganizing tendencies apparent in Solomon's reign continued.

So the years just before the entrance of the first of the classical prophets were characterized by division, economic and social upheaval, idolatry and numerous other manifestations of a near wholesale disregard of the covenant with the Lord. At this juncture Amos, then Hosea, appeared, to be followed by other prophets of God who would protest the abuses of the day and call Israel back to God, back to the covenant.

> When it was apparent that the nation as a whole had by its misconduct completely rebelled against Yahweh's rule . . . it was clear that some sterner word was called for. That word the classical prophets brought. Their entire attack on the sins of society was rooted in an overpowering sense of Yahweh's sovereign lordship over Israel, and of Israel's obligation unconditionally to obey the stipulations of his covenant.[8]

Motivated by a profound understanding of the covenant and

its requirements, the prophets pronounced God's judgment on Judah's and Israel's violation of it, their rebelliousness toward the Lord. Hence, these prophets were not religious innovators, delivering some new word from God. Instead, they held firmly to the normative traditions, taking to task all Israel and Judah for forsaking the faith.

Judgment and Hope

In the midst of spiritual deterioration and cultural upheaval God raised up spokesmen to proclaim a needed, fresh, forceful message. This message juxtaposed warning and encouragement, judgment and hope. The judgment theme is most pointed in the brief message Jonah delivered to the people of Nineveh: "Forty more days and Nineveh will be destroyed" (Jon 3:4). Yet destruction was not the final word, even for these non-Israelites: the Ninevites believed and repented—and God spared them from the threatened judgment (Jon 3:5-10).

The two-edged word, judgment and hope, is also seen in such prophets as Amos, Jeremiah and Ezekiel. For example, chapters one and two of Amos present, in recurring form, judgment first against Israel's neighbors, then against Israel and Judah. For each oracle there is an introduction, a brief description of the detestable present situation, and the pronouncement of judgment.

This is what the LORD says:
"For three sins of Judah,
     even for four, I will not turn back my wrath.
Because they have rejected the law of the LORD
     and have not kept his decrees,
because they have been led astray by false gods,
     the gods their ancestors followed,
I will send fire upon Judah
     that will consume the fortresses of Jerusalem."
(Amos 2:4-5)

But, even though most of Amos is given over to judgment,
its conclusion is a promise of salvation:

"I will plant Israel in their own land,
never again to be uprooted
from the land I have given them,"
says the LORD your God. (Amos 9:15; see also vv. 11-14)

Jeremiah earned the title "Prophet of Doom" by repeatedly
proclaiming the destruction facing Judah. The people had
broken the covenant; hence, the Lord was bringing upon
them an inescapable disaster (Jer 11:10-11). Though busy
with religious rites, the people were not walking in obedience,
nor did they listen to the word of the Lord (6:16-20; 7:21-26;
et al.). Therefore, judgment was just around the corner (6:21-
30; 7:27-29; et al.). Yet destruction was not the whole story:

"The days are coming," declares the LORD, "when I will
bring my people Israel and Judah back from captivity and
restore them to the land I gave their forefathers to possess."
"I am with you and will save you," declares the LORD.
"Though I completely destroy all the nations among which
I scatter you, I will not completely destroy you." (Jer 30:
3, 11)

Ezekiel, too, was a prophet of doom. His message characterized Jerusalem as an illegitimate child and prostitute (Ezek
16), and Israel as rebellious from the beginning (20:5-29).
In graphic language Ezekiel spoke out against Israel:

This is what the LORD says: I am against you. I will draw
my sword from its scabbard and cut off from you both the
righteous and the wicked. . . . My sword will be unsheathed
against everyone from south to north. (Ezek 21:3-4)

Yet the Lord would restore his people (34:25-31) and breathe
new life into them (37:1-14; see also 36:25-27).

A Call to Present Faithfulness

Through his prophets, the Lord communicated a message of
judgment for a people who disregarded the covenant, but one

of hope for the faithful. Often the prophetic message proclaimed a future judgment or salvation; however, we would be
badly mistaken if we concluded from this that the prophetic
message was directed only toward the future. The cutting
edge of the prophetic message was the *present*. Perhaps this is
most clearly seen in passages with an explicit "now" reference,
such as Joel 2:12-13:
> "Even now," declares the LORD,
>> "return to me with all your heart,
>> with fasting and weeping and mourning."
> Rend your heart and not your garments.
> Return to the LORD your God,
>> for he is gracious and compassionate,
>> slow to anger and abounding in love,
>> and he relents from sending calamity.

Tear out

Or in prophetic demands such as Amos 5:4-5:
> "Seek me and live;
>> do not seek Bethel,
> do not go to Gilgal,
>> do not journey to Beersheba."

Yet not only in such texts is the prophetic word directed to the
present. In an important sense, *all* the prophetic oracles were
directed at their own day. By means of warnings and encour-
agements regarding the *future*, all Israel was called to *present*
faithfulness. Hence, even the prophecies pointing to a seem-
ingly distant future were not primarily given to map out that
future. Quite the contrary—with references to tomorrow, the
prophets were calling for repentance today and for a present
renewed faith in a God who actively controls history.

In this context the inclusion among the prophets of the
book of Habakkuk, in which is found no "Thus says the
LORD," begins to make sense. His recorded experience underscores the idea of present faithfulness to the Lord even
(or especially!) when outward particulars raise doubts about
God's character and ability or existence.

Though the fig tree does not bud
    and there are no grapes on the vines,
though the olive crop fails
    and the fields produce no food,
though there are no sheep in the pen
    and no cattle in the stalls,
yet I will rejoice in the LORD,
    I will be joyful in God my Savior. (Hab 3:17-18)

More than ever before in Israel's history, the prophets, in their calls to present faithfulness, emphasized the rights and responsibilities of the individual. Heretofore in the history of God's relationship to Israel, the emphasis fell on the people as a whole, a chosen nation. But the nation was corrupt, under judgment. The later prophets encouraged individual men and women to be faithful to their Lord now, in the present, in view of the new community God would form in the future.

This discussion introduces the important distinction between prophecy as "foretelling" and as "forthtelling."[9] The prophet as "foreteller" is one who predicts a future happening. As "forthteller" the prophet announces or proclaims a message before a certain group or person. Of late, as at other points in the history of the church, there has been a widespread tendency to regard the prophets first and foremost as foretellers. Thus the prophetic writings are often regarded as gold mines from which to gather nuggets of futuristic import. Enough has been said already to raise serious questions about such interpretations, which do violence to the authors' intentions and their way of thinking.[10]

The prophet was ordinarily not concerned directly with the chronology of things to come. Rather, he "viewed the future as a great canvas of God's redemptive working in terms of height and breadth but lacking the clear dimension of depth."[11] That is, the present and future existed in tension; the immediate and ultimate future were not always clearly demarcated. Thus Zephaniah could speak of the Day of the Lord both in terms of Judah's historical disaster and in terms of the last day, the final judgment. In each case the focus of the message is on what God is doing, how he is fulfilling his purpose and promise.

Be that as it may, we cannot deny that the prophets, standing in the counsel of God, also saw a more distant horizon. While their special concern was present experience in the context of a longstanding, now forgotten, covenant with God, we must not overlook the predictive element of their message. To such future-looking announcements we will return in chapter eight.

Apocalyptic Writings

In its postexilic era, Israel began to experience an ebb in prophetic activity. This is hinted at already in Zechariah 1:4-5. The decline is reflected in 1 Maccabees, which traces Jewish history in the years 175-134 B.C. (4:46; 9:27; and 14:41). Later the Jewish historian Josephus would also note it (*Against Apion* 1.40-41). The period saw the waning of prophetic inspiration; however, speaking in broad terms, with the decline in prophetic activity, Israel saw the rise of an alternative means of revelation—that embodied in apocalyptic.[12]

Apocalyptic refers to three distinct, yet closely related phenomena: a form of literature, a religious perspective, and a religiously motivated social movement. We are particularly interested with these first two phenomena here.

"In its broadest sense, the word *apocalyptic* designates the disclosure through human agents of God's presence and activity, which would otherwise remain hidden from his people."[13] The word itself derives from the Greek word for "revelation," *apocalypsis*, used in the introduction to the book of Revelation (1:1). Apocalyptic, the progeny of crisis, was particularly prominent in the period from 200 B.C. to A.D. 100. Its gestation, however, can be traced earlier in such Old Testament prophetic texts as Isaiah 24—27, Ezekiel 37—38 and Zechariah 9—14. Its birth was the reaction to years of turmoil, years in which God's promises seemed to go unfulfilled, years in which God seemed to have abandoned his people. Where is God? When every evidence points to the contrary, can God be working out his redemptive plan? Apocalyptic was the fruit of just such questions answered in terms of a mighty, future intervention by God. In apocalyptic a hopeless people found new hope in a God who would vindicate his chosen and fulfill his purpose. The apocalyptic perspective was born and developed as emphasis on the transcendent—the future and spiritual—gradually replaced emphasis on the present and material. Apocalyptic saw history from the standpoint of God's overarching plan for all the world.

It is difficult to make general statements that are true for all apocalyptic literature because of the wide variety in these writings.[14] In distinguishing apocalyptic from prophecy, the most obvious difference concerns the means by which the message is communicated. The prophetic "word of the Lord" gives way to revelation through a vision or dream. Symbolism, imagery, numbers—seen already in prophetic texts—come to the fore with greater elaboration in apocalyptic. Apocalyptic texts sometimes reinterpret earlier prophecies; for example, Daniel refers to Jeremiah's "seventy years" in Daniel 9:2. Most important, though, is the difference in the focus of the message. The prophets proclaimed God's working in and through the course of history. The apocalyptists anticipated a radical intervention by God at the end, beyond history.

It should not, however, be concluded from this that present history was of no significance for apocalyptists. Quite the contrary, in the apocalyptic perspective the contemporary scene is the stage on which God's purpose is worked out. In this sense there is continuity between the "here" and the "hereafter."

It is true, nonetheless, that central to apocalyptic was the idea of two ages—the present age and the age to come. While the present age was not devoid of God's presence and activity, it was nevertheless doomed. Hope was concentrated on the age to come, the age instituted and ruled by God. Apocalyptists viewed the end of the present age as imminent.

Above all, apocalyptists were people of hope, trusting in a God who alone was sovereign. He alone was in control, moving history to its consummation, bringing deliverance to his faithful.

Usually regarded as the earliest apocalypse, Daniel is the only such book included in the Old Testament, though, as previously mentioned, apocalyptic features are visible in other parts of the Old Testament. The book of Daniel is widely known for its interpretive difficulties;[15] however, identifying it as an apocalyptic writing provides an important key to understanding its message. For Daniel and the people of his day, history raised critical questions: What is God doing? Why is he not actively intervening on behalf of his people in fulfillment of his promises? The book of Daniel seeks to answer such questions through dreams and visions, symbols and numbers. Anyone who wants to understand Daniel, then, does well to approach Daniel's writing seeking answers to these same questions. Not only does Daniel try to give his readers a divine perspective on the course and meaning of history, he also outlines what their present response to God should be. Like Habakkuk, Daniel calls for present faithfulness to God, even in the face of apparent abandonment. (Compare Habakkuk 3:14-19 with Daniel 3:16-18.) It is important to keep in mind that, although we will continue to follow common practice in referring to Daniel as a prophet, the literary form of his book is primarily apocalyptic rather than prophetic.

Elements of apocalyptic are also found in the New Testament,[16] both in Jesus' teaching[17] and in apostolic Christianity. By way of example we may point to Jesus' understanding and

expectation of a future kingdom of God—a development
from the apocalyptic concept of the new age. Moreover, the
idea of the resurrection, which owes its development in Israel
to apocalyptic, is presumed by Jesus. Early Christians interpreted Jesus' resurrection as the beginning of the general
resurrection of the dead (1 Cor 15:12-23). Moreover, the
early church continued the apocalyptic stress on the new age
in the guise of the kingdom of God, which was set in motion by
Jesus' ministry to be consummated at any moment by his return. In many ways early Christianity drew from the background of Jewish apocalyptic, but in their encounter with
Jesus apocalyptic lines of thought were transformed. Jesus—
his life, death and resurrection—was seen as the decisive point
in history, and the apocalyptic perspective was modified accordingly.

Mark 13 (see also Mt 24) also exemplifies the presence of
apocalyptic elements in New Testament thought. Indeed, this
chapter has often been entitled "The Little Apocalypse."
Although lacking certain qualities of apocalyptic writing, it
uses apocalyptic imagery and presents an apocalyptic message. In 13:4, four of Jesus' disciples ask him, in essence,
"When is the end?" Verses 5-31 might be regarded as paren-
thetical in that the real answer to their question comes only in
verse 32: "Only the Father knows." Rather than outlining a
chronological sequence of events leading up to the end, this
chapter proclaims an apocalyptic message with such features
as (1) an indication of the imminence of the end, (2) a warning of impending hardships, (3) an assurance of God's control over the course of history and (4) a call to believers to
maintain constant watchfulness. Mark 13 is properly understood only when viewed in relation to apocalyptic thought.

Our interest does not stop with New Testament apocalyptic, for in the New Testament we see the renewal of the prophetic office. New Testament prophets have much in common with their Old Testament counterparts.[18] First, Christian

prophets, like their Old Testament counterparts, are divinely called and inspired. They are prophets due to a special *charisma,* of spiritual endowment, from God. Second, Christian prophets function within the community of faith, particularly, but not necessarily, in the context of community worship. Third, Christian prophets present an intelligible message for the strengthening, encouragement and comfort of the church. We have only glimpses into the activity of Christian prophets in the New Testament—for example, in 1 Corinthians 14 and Acts 21:10-11.

The Revelation of John

The book of Revelation is the sole New Testament writing which claims to be prophecy (1:3; 22:7, 10, 18-19). As a prophet John communicates in written form the divine word (1:3; 2:1, 8, 12, 18; 3:1, 7, 14; 19:9; 22:7, 9-10, 18-19)—a task to which God called him (1:10-20; 10:8-10). The book, however, is also called a "revelation"—that is, an apocalypse (1:1)—and apocalyptic features pervade the writing. Visions, fantastic images, the emphasis on the imminence of the end, the ever-present assurance of God's sovereignty over events, the distinction between the present and the new age—all these apocalyptic elements can be found in Revelation.

Because of its apocalyptic-prophetic character, the book of Revelation is difficult to interpret.[19] The problem of imagery in prophecy and apocalyptic will be taken up in the next chapter. At this point we can only underscore two imperatives. First, the Revelation of John must be interpreted in view of the literary forms it uses. Instead of providing an end-time chart, John was seeking to communicate an important, divine message to his contemporaries. That the message of Revelation was very much oriented to the Christians of his own day is indicated by John's repeated admonition to them to keep the things written in the prophecy (1:3; 22:7). Furthermore, by giving the book the form of an epistle (see 1:4-5—the salutation; 22:21—the benediction), John reveals his intent to address his own people and underscores the gravity of his appeal. This point is all the more striking if we compare John's Revelation with the zenith of Jewish apocalyptic writings, the book of Enoch. In 1 Enoch 1:2 the author writes that what he saw, heard and understood was "not for this generation, but for a remote one which is to come."

Second, the Revelation of John must be viewed in its historical context, and with an attempt to understand each part of the book (for example, each vision) in the context of the whole.[20] The Revelation of John was written in a particular historical setting, many of the significant details of which can be collected by a careful reading of the book itself. Most evident is that the Christian churches to which John was writing had already begun to experience suffering (tribulation) at the hands of the state. Convinced that the present age was the last before the new age, the author proclaimed a message of hope to his audience. Though suffering must continue for a while longer, God would *certainly* vent his wrath on those who persecuted the church, who spilled the blood of the martyrs; and he would *certainly* bring in the new age. In this light the Revelation called Christians to faithfulness and hope. Or, as John put it, to Jesus' assurance, "Yes, I am coming soon," the Christian replies, "Amen. Come, Lord Jesus" (Rev 22:20).

Prophecy and apocalyptic—together making up what we popularly call "biblical prophecy"—are unique literary forms that require appropriate methods of interpretation. They are not straightforward proverbial sayings, nor pedagogy in college-lecture format, nor news stories in the Sunday morning paper—and they must not be approached as such. They are forms of communication chosen by God to reveal his nature and purpose in particular life-settings. In order to interpret their message in a valid way, we must become familiar with those life-settings and the forces which gave rise to this or that way of thinking. In this chapter we have briefly surveyed those formative currents and pointed to the prophetic and apocalyptic perspectives. Additionally, we have suggested important themes for which to look when interpreting biblical texts and have laid the groundwork for approaching the texts on their own terms.

6
Symbolism:
The Prophet's Tool

Four-headed beasts, seas of blood, bowls of wrath and froglike evil spirits—with such stuff must the interpreter of biblical prophecy be concerned.

Used already by the classical prophets, symbolism came to be a much-wielded tool for the apocalyptists who followed— Daniel and John. From early times to the present, the meaning of apocalyptic images and numbers, like those of the prophets, has been heavily disputed. Some have presumed to interpret the figures literally—anticipating, for example, an actual "woman sitting on a scarlet beast that was covered with blasphemous names and had seven heads and ten horns" (Rev 17:3). Others have sought allegorical interpretations, seeing in Daniel's reference to the "ten horns . . . from this kingdom" (7:24) the present-day European Economic Community. Still others have wondered if such fantastic images are capable of any explanation, rational or otherwise. Indeed, at the outset of the Reformation, Martin Luther explained his misgivings with the book of Revelation partly on the grounds that it was too much concerned with tales and pictures. In this chapter we will look into the purpose of symbolism for the prophets and apocalyptic writers and suggest appropriate guidelines for interpreting symbolic writings.

Images and Communication

First, an experiment: darken a room and light a candle. Gaze into its flame for a few moments, then close your eyes. You will still be able to "see" the flame, for its impression remains. It has left on your mind an image outliving the actual physical sight. Not only candles, but also words and ideas can leave imprints on our minds. Images stay with us long after specific words, written or spoken, have been lost. Who has not gone away from a sermon, having forgotten title and text, but remembering well that fabulous illustration? Words conjure up in our imagination pictures of things real and unreal, helping us grasp more clearly the thoughts being conveyed. Consider these three examples. What images do these words communicate?

Example 1: See Flip run. Run, Flip, run. Run. Run. Run.

Example 2: Suddenly the great beast beat its hideous wings, and the wind of them was foul. Again it leaped into the air, and then swiftly fell down upon Eowyn, shrieking, striking with beak and claw.

Still she did not blench: maiden of the Rohirrim, child of kings, slender but as a steel-blade, fair yet terrible. A swift stroke she dealt, skilled and deadly. The outstretched neck she clove asunder, and the hewn head fell like a stone. Backward she sprang as the huge shape crashed to ruin, vast wings outspread, crumpled on the earth; and with its fall the shadow passed away. A light fell about her, and her hair shone in the sunrise.[1]

Example 3: And I saw a beast coming out of the sea. He had ten horns and seven heads, with ten crowns on his horns, and on each head a blasphemous name. The beast I saw resembled a leopard, but had feet like those of a bear and a mouth like that of a lion. . . . One of the heads of the beast seemed to have had a fatal wound, but the fatal wound had been healed.[2]

Example 1 is reminiscent of a first-grade text. It offers little in itself as a means of communication. In order to imagine its message, we must provide the details it leaves out. If Flip is a dog (and here we are not told so), what kind? What color? Long hair or short? How graceful? How fast? Why does Flip run? What is the scenic background? And so on. Example 2 comes from the renowned fantasy classic by J. R. R. Tolkien, *The Lord of the Rings*. Tolkien here reveals his ability to breathe life into a story. His words paint a picture for the reader; the scene almost leaps off the page and becomes a Technicolor production. The third example is the handiwork of John, author of Revelation. His words also command our creative thought, drawing forth fantastic images. With picturesque language John landscapes his message.

Modern communication theory holds that we understand and retain far more of what we see than what we only hear or read. Hence, today's public speakers often use graphs, maps, overhead projectors and a host of other audio-visual aids. Writers, however, depend only on the written word to communicate their images. They do not generally sell a package of transparencies along with their tomes. They rely solely on their use of language to cause the reader to smell, see, hear—to experience their words. Neither could the prophets of old rely on modern communication paraphernalia. Instead, they embraced symbolism in word and deed to highlight and illustrate their divine communiqués. Symbolism is, above all, a communication device.

So there is nothing to be gained by reading Revelation as a theological essay such as Paul might have written or as a historical narrative of the kind found in Acts. "It is a word of a different sort: an acted word, a word dramatized, painted, set to music—a word you can see and feel and taste."[3] The same can be said for the book of Daniel and much of the other prophetic writings.

Along with proclaiming the divine word, prophets in both Testaments used symbolic actions to dramatize their messages. Symbolic deeds took many forms. Jeremiah remained unmarried in order to indicate the abnormality of the times (16:1-4). Hosea gave his children names with symbolic import (1:4, 6, 9). By far the most common pattern of prophetic-symbolic deed, however, was the acting out of a prophetic word. Acts 21 relates just such a story:

> A prophet named Agabus came down from Judea. Coming over to us, he took Paul's belt, tied his own hands and feet with it and said, "The Holy Spirit says, 'In this way the Jews of Jerusalem will bind the owner of this belt and will hand him over to the Gentiles.' " (vv. 10-11)

In the Old Testament are many illustrations of this phenomenon. One example is the narrative of Isaiah 20:

> At that time the LORD spoke through Isaiah son of Amoz. He said to him, "Take off the sackcloth from your body and the sandals from your feet." And he did so, going around stripped and barefoot.
>
> Then the LORD said, "Just as my servant Isaiah has gone stripped and barefoot for three years, as a sign and portent against Egypt and Cush, so the king of Assyria will lead away stripped and barefoot the Egyptian captives and Cushite exiles, young and old, with buttocks bared—to Egypt's shame." (vv. 2-4)

These examples reveal how the prophets combined deeds with the spoken word, the verbal message bringing out the significance of the symbolic. Once understood, symbolic deeds provided a vivid, concrete reminder of the divine message.[4]

In their symbolic language, the biblical prophets primarily

used symbols taken from the ordinary world. Micah 5:7-8, for example, describes the remnant of Jacob in figurative language as "dew from the LORD," "showers on the grass," "a lion among the beasts of the forest," "a young lion among flocks of sheep." At times the prophet would engage particularly extravagant language to create a more forceful image, as in Jeremiah 4:23-24:

I looked at the earth,
    and it was formless and empty;
and at the heavens,
    and their light was gone.
I looked at the mountains,
    and they were quaking;
    all the hills were swaying.

As with much of the prophetic books, these two examples are poetic in form—a fact of no little consequence for the interpreter. Hebrew poetry consistently balances thought against thought, word against word, and a basic familiarity with such parallelism is fundamental to understanding its message.[5] There are three main types of parallelism:

1. *Synonymous* parallelism, in which the second line repeats the thought of the first. Isaiah 48:19 illustrates this category, with line 2 matching the sense of line 1, and line 4 matching line 3.

Your descendants would have been like the sand,
    your children like its numberless grains;
their name would never be cut off
    nor destroyed from before me.

2. *Antithetical* parallelism, in which the first line is balanced by the second through contrast of thought, as in Hosea 7:14:

They do not cry out to me from their hearts
    but wail upon their beds.

3. *Synthetic* parallelism, in which the second element advances the thought of the first, providing additional descriptive material, as in Obadiah 21:

Deliverers will go up on Mount Zion
   to govern the mountains of Esau.
And the kingdom will be the LORD's.
Parallelism is very much a mark of Old Testament poetry. Attention to its occurrence and type in the prophets will go far in
allowing for a proper interpretation.

The Hebrew prophets, whether using poetry or not, ordinarily drew images from the real world in their employment
of symbolism. Clay in the hand of the potter (Jer 18:6), the
diet of locusts (Joel 2:25), rough country made smooth (Is 40:
4)—all come from everyday life. The apocalyptic writers, on
the other hand, lead us into the realm of fantasy, of images
drawn from the creative imagination. Not all, but a good
many, of the symbols used in Daniel and Revelation belong to
a sphere beyond reality: the beasts of Daniel 7 and the dragon
of Revelation 12, to give only two illustrations. How should
these be interpreted?

Before listing interpretive suggestions, let us briefly sum-
marize the prophets' reasons for using symbolism. We have
already mentioned the desire to dramatize the prophetic
word. Symbolism sometimes was used to embody the divine
message. Thus did Hosea's marriage to the adulterous Gomer
symbolize the relationship between God and his people. In
addition, symbolism was used to speak of realities beyond
human descriptive experience. How can we speak of heaven,
except with some sort of picture-language (such as that in
Revelation 21)? Symbolic language, then, points to something
real, but its images are not the reality itself.

Principles for Interpreting Symbolism
With this in mind we now turn to consider five principles for
interpreting the symbolism of biblical prophecy. We are em-
phasizing the apocalyptic writers because their language most
acutely raises the interpretive problem.

1. Approach symbolism with humility. Upon describing his

vision, Daniel remarks: "I, Daniel, was exhausted and lay ill for several days. Then I got up and went about the king's business. I was appalled by the vision; it was beyond understanding" (8:27). While we may respond to Daniel's vision less with exhaustion than with perplexity, we easily identify with his concluding comment: "it was beyond understanding." The simple fact is that there is much symbolism recorded by the canonical apocalyptic writers—Daniel and John—about which we can only speculate. We can be confident that the symbols communicated something intelligible to the original audiences of the biblical writers, but in some cases the key to understanding is lost to modern readers. Let us therefore not be overly dogmatic about our reconstructions of the meanings of such symbolic writings.

2. *Recognize the primacy of imagination over reason.* It is no use approaching much of the prophetic Scriptures as if they were a theological treatise. The important key for unlocking the mysteries of fantastic symbolism is not logical analysis. Rather, we must train ourselves to think in pictures, to view Revelation's visions as if they were in picture-book form or in a feature film. As we shall see, this does not negate rational thought. Before we analyze, however, we must *see* what is going on.

3. *Find the meaning in context.* A common axiom for biblical interpretation is simply stated: Interpret Scripture with Scripture. What seems opaque at one juncture is often explained with great clarity elsewhere in the Bible. This axiom is frequently used in interpreting the symbolic language of Revelation.[6] At first sight, this makes sense. After all, a great deal of the imagery found in Revelation can be traced back to the Old Testament. Moreover, a necessary first step for interpreting Revelation's pictures is to determine their background in the Old Testament or elsewhere.[7] However, one should never think this first step concludes the process. It is not necessarily true that what a given symbol meant for Ezekiel will also be its significance for John. John may be using images which

parallel those in the Old Testament or some other ancient tradition, but in an amended way. We must ask a further question, then: How does *John* use this symbol?

At times the author of Revelation explicitly states the meaning of his symbolic language. The "one like a son of man" (from Dan 7:13) is clearly Christ Jesus—the one who was dead, but who now lives for ever and ever (Rev 1:12-18). John identifies the great dragon as Satan (Rev 12:9). The prostitute of Revelation 17 is "the great city" (v. 18), a reference to Rome.[8] Interpretations which John himself provides should be adhered to closely and taken as the point of departure for the understanding of other symbols.

One illustration of John's use of an Old Testament image is found in chapter 13. John describes "a beast coming out of the sea," having ten horns and seven heads. This beast is called forth and empowered by the dragon (Satan) to war against the church. John's portrayal of this beast unmistakably identifies it with the fourth (and last) empire of Daniel's vision of the end (Dan 7). John's use of the symbol, however, goes beyond Daniel's. This is clear first in that John combines in this one figure elements from each of Daniel's kingdom-beasts. Moreover, John reveals that he has in mind one empire, represented by, or embodied in, *one ruler*. Additionally, John introduces here a second beast unknown to Daniel's vision, a figure from the earth whose task was to cause people to worship the first beast or be killed. John wishes to make clear that these two beasts are the instruments of Satan and that to worship the beast is to bend the knee to Satan.

How would John's first readers have understood these images? Already in New Testament times, the emperor of Rome was increasingly seen not only as an agent of the gods, but as a god himself. For many, the emperor was the deity who guaranteed sustenance and fulfillment in life. Thus he was to be worshiped *as a god*. This state of affairs constituted no small problem for Christians, who gave their highest allegiance to their Lord and who looked to him, not to the Roman emperor, for daily provision. As this imperial religion developed further, the state would harass Christians more and more, pressing them to renounce Christ in favor of emperor worship. In such a context, the beast from the sea would have symbolized the deified emperor. His counterpart from the earth would have represented those persons—priests, philosophers, and the like—who promoted the imperial religion.

4. Look for the prophet's pastoral concern. In giving this example, we have already been reminded of a much-sung theme of this book—namely, that John's concern (like that of the other biblical prophets) was more for his own congregations and the situations they were facing than for a future epoch. This pastoral emphasis is exhibited in Revelation 13:9-10:

He who has an ear, let him hear.
If anyone is to go into captivity,
   into captivity he will go.
If anyone is to be killed with the sword,
   with the sword he will be killed.
This calls for patient endurance and faithfulness on the
   part of the saints.

In calling his readers to steadfastness (see also 2:10; 14:12), John clearly reveals his pastoral concern; his own contemporaries are uppermost in his mind. Hence, we must not neglect the historical contexts of the various writings in our fervor to find "fulfilled prophecy."

5. Look for the main point. Apocalyptic writers employ visions for much the same reason that Jesus taught in parables—to drive home in a dramatic, memorable fashion one significant point. So, when we are interpreting Daniel or Revelation, we must consider whole pictures just as we study parables in their entirety. The interpreter's task is to uncover the leading idea of the vision, the main point, and not to squeeze from every detail some allegorical meaning. Details serve mainly to supply the panoramic background for the main event, either for dramatic effect or to fill in necessary points of reference.[9]

Look again at the description of the beast from the sea in Revelation 13. Certain of the details identify the beast with the last kingdom of Daniel's vision. Other details show this beast to be Satan's counterpart to the Christ of God:[10]

The Beast from the Sea	Christ Jesus
Ten crowns (13:1)	Many crowns (19:12)
Blasphemous names (13:1)	Names: "Faithful," "True," "Word of God, "KING OF KINGS AND LORD OF LORDS" (19:11, 13, 16)
Power, throne and authority of Satan (13:2)	Power, throne and authority of God (12:5, 10)
A death-wound, healed (13:3)	Having died, he lives (1:18; see also 5:6)
Causes people to worship Satan (13:4)	Causes people to worship God (1:6; et al.)

In this case, the details only underscore what is already quite plain: the beast is Satan's agent of war against Christians. John's purpose here is to tell his people that the present persecution has its origins with the devil, that to renounce the Lord to worship the emperor is to embrace Satan himself. Then, in this light, he calls the saints to faithfulness.

John's message to his own people, of course, has relevance for our own day just as it does for every Christian age. We must be cautious, though, about how we explain that relevance. John has used symbols to convey his message; the symbols, however, are not *the* message. To translate John's message to our own day does not require finding detail-for-detail correspondence between John's symbols and our present circumstances. (Trying to locate a person with a fatal head-wound which has been healed is therefore a moot exercise.) Rather, once we find the point of John's message for his contemporaries, we can translate that point to our own setting.

In fact, John's images were greater than his historical context. That is, when John wrote of the beast from the sea who had power to cause persons to worship him, and to war against the saints and conquer them, the point of his message extended beyond the difficulties associated with the worldly kingdom of his own day. Symbolized was the essential character of any worldly kingdom which adopts an antagonistic stance toward the Christian faith. John, then, speaks to us a pastoral message—an encouragement to faithfulness, a reminder that God will ultimately triumph and vindicate his saints, and a stern warning about worshiping any but Jesus as Lord. If this summary seems to lack the drama and urgency of John's communiqué, is it not because we know so little about persecution for the faith?

A Note on Numbers

Many so-called solutions to problems relating to the end have resulted from calculating dates and periods from biblical numbers. The seventy sevens (weeks?) of Daniel 9:24 and the thousand years (millennium) of Revelation 20:1-6 are frequently used this way. How are these and other biblical numbers best understood?

First, we should recall that the ancients were not nearly as concerned with numerical accuracy as we have become. Checking attendance, constructing flow charts, counting change, filling in Internal Revenue Service tax forms—these and many similar exercises have rendered our present society highly sensitive to exactness in figuring. It was not so for people of old. They were much more interested in statistical approximations and the symbolic meanings of numbers.[11]

For example, consider this interpretation by Philo, a contemporary of the apostle Paul, of the six and seven days of the Genesis creation account:

When, then, [Moses] says, "He finished his work on the sixth day," we should understand him to be adducing not a fullness of days, but a perfect number: six. . . . Thus [Moses]

wished to exhibit alike the things created of mortal kind and
those that are incorruptible as having been formed in a way
corresponding to their proper numbers. As I have said, he
makes mortal things parallel with the number six, and the
happy and blessed things with the number seven. (*Legum
Allegoria* 1.4)

It is true that Philo's allegorical understanding of numbers
and events goes far beyond that discovered in the Bible;
nevertheless, his writing typifies a general attitude regarding
the significance attached to numbers in antiquity.

The number forty, for example, carries special, symbolic
meaning in the Old and New Testaments. Forty days or years
is often associated with critical situations—such as a time of
judgment (Gen 7:4), a period for fasting (Deut 9:9) and test-
ing (Mt 4:2), or a time for repentance (Jon 3:4). Three, on the
other hand, suggests completeness (see Num 6:24-26; Dan 6:
10; 1 Jn 5:8).

Apocalyptic writers in particular made use of symbolic
numbers, such as the ten horns of the beast (Dan 7:7, 20, 24;
Rev 12:3; 13:1; 17:3, 7, 12, 16). Daniel's stress on the symbolic meaning of numbers shows itself in 9:24-27 (see 9:2),
where he indicates that Jeremiah's reference to the seventy
years was not to be taken at face value. Even if the numbers in
Daniel 8:14; 9:2, 24-27; and 12:11-12 did not occur in an
apocalyptic setting, even if they were intended literally, it
would be difficult to make any literal sense of them.

Second, we must not overlook the fact that neither Jesus
nor the early church (as far as we know) made any attempts
to prove Jesus' messiahship with reference to biblical mathematics. Given the importance of the Old Testament in demonstrating the messianic significance of Jesus' person and ministry (see chapter seven), this omission is certainly odd if the
prophetic numbers were intended to be understood literally.
And third, as we will see in chapter eight, when asked by a
disciple to date the time of the end, Jesus promptly changed

the subject. He purposely directed the attention of his listeners away from timetables and date setting and taught them instead how they must live in the period before the end.

Hence, to treat the biblical texts in general, and the apocalyptic writings in particular, as a beachhead from which to launch eschatological timetables is to do them violence.[12]

The suggestions in this chapter are only guidelines for making sense of the fantastic figures found in biblical prophecy. For detailed assistance on the background of individual symbols, one will want to refer to the Bible dictionaries and commentaries recommended earlier. Of course, using these reference works is no substitute for carefully reading the biblical texts themselves. Such reading will often turn up important interpretive clues.

Still, discerning what the biblical authors had in mind with their employment of various symbols is often an elusive problem. Be that as it may, it remains imperative that in interpreting the prophetic Scriptures we make every effort to understand the *authors'* intentions. After all, symbols were instruments of communication aimed by the prophets and apocalyptists at their own contemporaries. To seek out correspondences between their symbolism and our newspapers' front pages is to miss the point entirely. Indeed, any attempt to proclaim the significance of the words of the prophets for our own day before understanding their historical significance is ill conceived.

7
Prophecy and Jesus

One of the most notable features of the New Testament is the extent to which it draws on the Old Testament, either by quotation or allusion. In particular, with dozens of references to the Old Testament, early Christian writers sought to demonstrate that Jesus was in fact the Messiah (or the Christ). Many details of Jesus' life, ministry and relationship to God were seen by those first disciples as fulfillment of Old Testament prophecies.[1] It is not surprising that a very old, traditional statement about the work of Christ explicitly asserts that what Jesus accomplished was in line with the Old Testament:

Christ died for our sins
according to the Scriptures, . . .
he was buried [and] . . . was raised on the third day
according to the Scriptures, . . .
he appeared to Peter, and then to the Twelve.
(1 Cor 15:3-5)

The opening chapters of Matthew illustrate well the use of the Old Testament to indicate Jesus' significance as the Christ.[2]

Matthew 1:1-17 asserts Jesus' Jewish pedigree and reveals
him as the climax of Old Testament history. Even more
pointedly, the story of Jesus' birth and early life (1:18—2:23)
declares that Jesus is the fulfillment of Old Testament expectations. First, Joseph is informed that Mary's pregnancy is
the work of the Spirit and that her offspring will save the people from their sins. The angelic message is underscored by a
reference to the prophecy of a son, Immanuel, born to a virgin (Mt 1:22-23; Is 7:14). Then Matthew points out that Jesus
was born in Bethlehem, foretold to be the birthplace of the
Messiah (Mt 2:1-6; Mic 5:2). Third, the story of Joseph and
Mary's flight with the baby Jesus to Egypt concludes with the
depiction of this event as fulfillment of prophecy (Mt 2:13-15;
Hos 11:1). Fourth, Herod's order to kill Bethlehem's male
children is considered the fulfillment of Jeremiah's words
concerning Rachel's weeping for her children (Mt 2:16-18;
Jer 31:15). Fifth, the family's return to Nazareth (Mt 2:19-23)
is said to be fulfillment of the prophetic word about the Messiah being called a Nazarene.[3] In each of these circumstances,
Jesus is revealed as the One about whom the prophets spoke.

Already, however, a problem of interpretation has arisen.
We have maintained that biblical prophecy must be viewed
against its historical context in relation to the purpose intended by the original author. Yet Matthew uses a nonpredic-
tive statement—Hosea 11:1, a historical reference to the
exodus—as though it were a predictive prophecy concerning
the Messiah. The same kind of problem arises with his use of
Isaiah 7:14 and Jeremiah 31:15.

And Matthew is not the only culprit; other New Testament
writers speak of the "fulfillment" of what are, in fact, non-
predictive sayings—texts which anticipate no fulfillment.
Several New Testament writers treat the "royal psalms" (for
example, Psalms 2, 18, 20, 21, 45, 72, 101, 110) as predictive
prophecies. Yet these psalms were originally formulated with
reference to particular historical kings. In the beginning they

did not refer to a future king, nor to a coming Messiah, but expressed the hopes of the people for the current reigning monarchy.[4] Nevertheless, in the New Testament they are cited as eschatological texts awaiting fulfillment. Psalm 2:7 ("You are my Son; today I have become your Father") is cited in Acts 13:33 and Hebrews 1:5; 5:5 as proof of Jesus' divine sonship. Psalm 110:1 ("The LORD says to my Lord: 'Sit at my right hand until I make your enemies a footstool for your feet' ") is quoted in Acts 2:34-35 to indicate the exaltation and lordship of Jesus. And Psalm 110:4 ("You are a priest forever, in the order of Melchizedek") is used in Hebrews 7:17 to demonstrate Christ's eternal priesthood. Yet these texts were not originally meant to be predictions of the coming agent of God's salvation. How could the New Testament writers interpret the Old Testament in (as it might appear to us) such arbitrary fashion?

Simply put, the answer lies in the perspective of the New Testament writers. The lens through which they viewed the Old Testament texts led them to interpret those texts in some remarkable ways. Their perspective was determined partly by the views of contemporary Jews, but even more so, and decisively, by the impact of their encounter with Jesus and their experience of the reality of resurrection life.

The New Testament writers shared an important presupposition with Jesus and many of their Jewish contemporaries about the Jewish Scriptures: The Old Testament, they thought, is anticipatory in nature. Throughout the Old Testament runs the persistent motif of a God faithful to his word. Because the Lord first reveals his promises, then fulfills them, Old Testament history came to be seen in terms of promise-fulfillment. "Yet each such event makes Israel look the more to the future for this pattern of experience to continue, so that each fulfillment in the past becomes promise for the future."[5] So there was ever-growing expectation, made explicit by the prophets, that even as God had delivered his people in the past, even as he had been faithful in the past, so would he act faithfully in the future. Moreover, because God had been faithful in the past, Israel refused to forget those promises which had not yet come to fruition. Trusting in God's ability to accomplish what he had promised, Israel projected unfulfilled promises into the future, to generations to come—even to the eschaton. Thus the Old Testament can be described as "a book of ever-increasing anticipation."[6]

The future hope of Israel took many forms. Most centered directly on the work of God. The Lord himself would respond and bring restoration (Hos 2:16-23); he would establish Zion (Is 14:32). Says the Sovereign Lord:

I will contend with those who contend with you,
   and your children *I* will save.
I will make your oppressors eat their own flesh;
   they will be drunk on their own blood, as with wine.
Then all mankind will know
   that *I*, the LORD, am your Savior,
   your Redeemer, the Mighty One of Jacob. (Is 49:25-26)

In addition to eschatological hopes for the Lord God's direct intervention and salvation, much testimony in the Old Testament and later Jewish literature points to a personal mediator or agent of God's salvation. While the Old Testament uses a number of titles and ideas to designate this savior-figure, *Messiah* came into use as a technical term for this mediator only in post-Old Testament times, in the intertestamental period.[7] By the time of Jesus, *Messiah* designated a future savior or redeemer in various guises. A brief survey of the three most important Messiah figures will illustrate how the forward-looking character of the Old Testament gave rise to such speculation. Also, it will provide a backdrop for seeing how Jesus related himself to such expectations.

Messianic Figures and Future Hopes
At the beginning of the first Christian century, Jewish mes-

sianic hope pointed predominantly to a King Messiah of David's lineage.[8] This expectation is rooted in 2 Samuel 7: 12-16, the record of God's promise to David of an eternal kingship. The course of history did not see this promise fulfilled in a literal way; the time came when David's throne no longer existed. The promise, however, was not forgotten. During the exile it was projected into the future, to a time of restoration: " 'In that day,' declares the LORD Almighty, ... 'they will serve the LORD their God and David their king, whom I will raise up for them' " (Jer 30:8-9). Ezekiel, too, proclaimed the restoration of a united Israel under one king, David (37:21-28).

From later, nonbiblical Jewish literature comes reliable evidence that the hope of a King Messiah flourished in the period before and during Jesus' earthly ministry. The Psalms of Solomon—named after, but not written by, King Solomon —are especially significant. This work is a collection of poems dating from the mid-first century B.C. The community from which these psalms originated anticipated the coming of the long-awaited son of David who would expel the foreign Roman government from Palestine and establish his own rule.

> Behold, O Lord, raise up for them their king, the son of
> David,
>> in the time which you know, O God,
>>> to reign over Israel your servant;
>> and gird him with strength to shatter the unjust rulers. ...
> He will possess the nations, to serve beneath his yoke;
>> he will glorify the Lord with the praise of all the earth.
> He will cleanse Jerusalem in holiness, as it was of old,
>> that the nations may come from the ends of the earth to
>>> see his glory,
>>> bearing as gifts her sons who had fainted,
>>> and to see the Lord's glory with which God has
>>>> glorified her.
> A righteous king, taught by God, is their ruler,

and there will be no unrighteousness among them all
    his days;
for all will be holy, and their king is the anointed Lord.[9]
The Messiah ("Anointed") was to be a king of David's lineage,
one who would not only restore Israel but also subject the nations ("Gentiles") to his rule. His would be a political *and* religious rule.

Further evidence for this line of messianic hope can be
found in the spoken, Aramaic translations of the Hebrew Old
Testament (called *targums*) used in regular Jewish synagogue
services.[10] Often, these translations incorporated surprising
nuances of interpretation, providing, as it were, a running
commentary on the passages being read. For example, Numbers 24:17, in the Hebrew Bible, reads: "A star shall come out
of Jacob and a scepter shall arise from Israel." But an Aramaic
translation reads, "A king shall arise from Jacob and a Messiah from Israel shall be installed." Note how the Targum
changes "star" and "scepter" to "king" and "Messiah," thus
spelling out an interpretation of the text along the lines of a
clear messianic hope. Another interesting example is Micah
5:2 (or 5:1 in the Hebrew manuscript) quoted by the chief
priests and scribes to King Herod to tell the birthplace of the
Messiah (Mt 2:5). Below, the translations are placed side by
side for comparison.

Hebrew Bible	*Aramaic Targum*
But you, Bethlehem Ephrathah,	But you, Bethlehem Ephratha,
insignificant among the clans of Judah,	as one who is counted small among the clans of the house of Judah,
from you shall come forth for me a ruler in Israel	from you shall come forth before me a Messiah who will exercise dominion over Israel
whose origins are from of old, from ancient times.	whose name was said from the first, from ancient times.

In the Aramaic interpretation, the indefinite "ruler in Israel" is spelled out explicitly: the one who will rule is the Messiah. The phrase "whose origins are from of old" is an allusion to the Davidic monarchy; hence, the text is a throwback to 2 Samuel 7.

Generally, then, "the Anointed One," in post-Old Testament times, meant the Davidic king. He was to be a descendant of David, one in whom God's promise to David of an eternal throne would be fulfilled. For this reason, he also bore the title "Son of David."

Another figure of the expected agent of God was the Prophet Messiah. We have already mentioned the development of this hope, rooted in the prophet like Moses of Deuteronomy 18:15-18. John 6:14-15 provides evidence that some people in Jesus' day anticipated the coming of the Prophet: "After the people saw the miraculous sign that Jesus did, they began to say, 'Surely this is the Prophet who is to come into the world.'" The writings of the pious Jewish sect at Qumran also point to a hope in a coming Prophet. The sect collected a selection of messianic proof-texts, and that anthology included the Deuteronomy passage about the prophet like Moses. Additionally, according to the *Rule of the Community,* the men at Qumran envisaged the appearance of the Prophet.[11]

The final figure of importance for understanding messianic expectations in pre-Christian Judaism is the Priest Messiah. This conception was foreshadowed in Psalm 110:4 ("You are a priest forever, in the order of Melchizedek") and in Zechariah 6:12-13:

> Tell him this is what the LORD Almighty says: "Here is the man whose name is the Branch, and he will branch out from his place and build the temple of the LORD. It is he who will build the temple of the LORD, and he will be clothed with majesty and will sit and rule on his throne. And he will be a priest on his throne. And there will be harmony between the two."

Both these Old Testament texts show glimpses of the priestly figure only in conjunction with the royal. Speculation about a Priest Messiah gained strength during the last two centuries B.C. At that time Jewish political autonomy was regained by priestly rulers, descendants of the house of Levi. (Psalm 110:4, which speaks of the order not of Levi but of Melchizedek, was not in focus in this brand of speculation.) One Jewish writing of this period, the Testament of Levi, anticipates a great, eschatological, priestly figure:

Then the Lord will raise up a new priest
    to whom all the words of the Lord will be revealed;
he will execute true judgment on the earth for a multitude
    of days.
His star will rise in heaven like that of a king,
    lighting up the light of knowledge like the midday sun. . . .
The heavens will be opened
    and from the temple of glory sanctification will come
        upon him
    with the Father's voice as from Abraham to Isaac. (18:2-6)

The texts from Qumran mentioned earlier also speak of a Priest Messiah.

With this brief survey of three significant messianic figures, the King, the Prophet and the Priest, it is clear how Old Testament promises, unfulfilled in their own historical contexts, spawned future hopes. Each expectation we have considered is based in the Old Testament, if only in skeletal form. As those figures were idealized and projected into the eschatological future, expectations associated with each were developed, even transformed. But what use did Jesus make of these messianic ideas, and how were his disciples thus influenced in their attitude to the Old Testament?[12]

Jesus and Messianic Expectations

The most characteristic attitude of Jesus toward the Old Testament was that the Old Testament found its culmination in his person. The motif of fulfillment—"What was written is now fulfilled"—frequently comes to center stage in Jesus' teaching. Luke 4:16-21 is a classic example of this kind of interpretation. In this text, Jesus enters the synagogue in his home town, Nazareth, and reads the lesson from the prophet Isaiah. The text he reads is Isaiah 61:1-2, perhaps the earliest interpretation of the Servant of the Lord.[13]

> The Spirit of the Lord is on me, because he has anointed me
>   to preach good news to the poor.
> He has sent me to proclaim freedom for the prisoners and
>   recovery of sight for the blind,
>   to release the oppressed,
>   to proclaim the year of the Lord's favor. (Lk 4:18-19)

Having completed the reading, Jesus rolled up the scroll, sat down to speak and then proclaimed, "Today this scripture is fulfilled in your hearing."

This same idea is explicit in John 5:39-47 where Jesus denounces the Pharisees. The passage reaches its climax with these words of Jesus: "If you believed Moses, you would believe me, for he wrote about me" (v. 46). These two texts, along with many others, clearly reveal Jesus' view of himself as the consummation of the Old Testament.[14] It is important to note, however, that while Jesus proclaimed himself the realization of Old Testament hope, he was not the Messiah for which late Judaism was waiting.

We have seen that at the beginning of the first century A.D. the one messianic expectation which overshadowed all other speculations focused on a King Messiah, the son of David. The concept of a King Messiah included ideas of political rulership, military conquest, national supremacy and earthly power. Nothing could be further from the Messiah picture given us by Jesus. In fact, owing to its nuances in popular usage, throughout his ministry Jesus refused to use the title *Messiah* in regard to himself. Even at Peter's confession, "You are the Christ," Jesus interpreted his messianic role in terms of suffering and rejection, not royalty and conquest (Mk 8:27-31). And, at his trial, when pointedly asked, "Are you the Christ?" Jesus evades the question, answers obliquely and alludes to the Son of Man from Daniel 7:13 (Mk 14:61-62; Lk 22:67-70). From the sparse evidence available to us, we may conclude that Jesus' notion of messiahship was set in sharp contrast to the expectations popular in his day. Nevertheless, because in Jesus' person God's reign was instituted, the designation *Messiah* very much belongs to him.

Jesus saw himself as the fulfillment of the Old Testament. Likewise, his first disciples were convinced that he was God's Messiah. (Indeed, *Christ* soon became attached to Jesus as a proper name.) Early Christians were convinced that the hope based in the Jewish Scriptures was realized in Jesus' person and work. This belief revolutionized their approach to interpreting those Scriptures. Not only did they apply to Jesus (and to themselves as God's people) the words of the Hebrew prophets, they also began to trace connections between Jesus and Old Testament persons and events. Known as typology, this way of viewing the Old Testament "expresses most clearly the basic attitude of primitive Christianity toward the Old Testament."[15]

Typology and prophecy are related in that both underscore the basic continuity between past and present. Prophecy, however, sees this continuity in terms of a forward look, a prediction demanding a future fulfillment. Typology involves a retrospective view, looking back and recognizing previous events or persons corresponding to the present state of affairs.

Typology is not allegory, since typology is grounded in facts, in history. Typology requires a real, historical correspondence between past and present. No such correspondence is necessary for allegorical interpretation, where words, names, events, even minor details are accorded a spiritual significance far outrunning the intended sense of the Old

Testament texts. In allegory, words become metaphors with hidden meaning.

Already Jesus had used Old Testament persons as types of himself—for example, "as Jonah was three days and three nights in the belly of a huge fish, so the Son of Man will be three days and three nights in the heart of the earth" (Mt 12:40-41). Paul expresses Jesus' significance in terms of Old Testament history in his well-known Adam-Christ typology (Rom 5:12-21). Matthew, too, uses typology, such as in his application of Isaiah 7:14 ("the virgin will . . . give birth to a son") to Jesus (Mt 1:22-23). Jesus was understood to represent Israel, so Hosea 11:1 ("out of Egypt I called my son [Israel]") could be typologically related to Jesus (Mt 2:15). Clearly, then, the early church, following Jesus' lead, mined the Old Testament to discover prophecies and patterns of Jesus' life and work because they were convinced that he was the culmination of Israel's history of salvation.

Jesus and Old Testament Interpretation
We can see now how the early Christians' attitude toward the Old Testament was decisively determined by their encounter with Jesus. Their foremost exegetical presupposition was that Christ is the focal point for Old Testament interpretation. He is the "Divine Yes"—"for no matter how many promises God has made, they are 'Yes' in Christ" (2 Cor 1:20). In his study *The New Testament Development of Old Testament Themes*, F. F. Bruce summarizes this idea:

> In Jesus the promise is confirmed, the covenant is renewed, the prophecies are fulfilled, the law is vindicated, salvation is brought near, sacred history has reached its climax, the perfect sacrifice has been offered and accepted, the great priest over the household of God has taken his seat at God's right hand, the Prophet like Moses has been raised up, the Son of David reigns, the kingdom of God has been inaugurated, the Son of Man has received dominion from the

Ancient of Days, the Servant of the Lord, having been smitten to death for his people's transgression and borne the sin of many, has accomplished the divine purpose, has seen the light after the travail of his soul and is now exalted and extolled and made very high.[16]

The Old Testament, then, helps us understand who Christ Jesus is. It provides the background without which much of the New Testament would be unexplainable. The titles of Jesus—Christ, Son of Man, Servant, Son of God, Lord, Word and Savior (to name the most prevalent)—all have a pre-history in the Old Testament. Their Old Testament usage fills them with content and, to a large extent, determines their meaning in the New Testament. Likewise, New Testament words used in explaining the effects of Jesus' ministry —salvation, deliverance, and so on—must be understood against the backdrop of God's dealings with his people in Old Testament times.

To understand Jesus as the Messiah of God, we must grasp the Old Testament anticipatory hope. We must understand Old Testament events, such as the Flood, in themselves before we can view them as types of the present work of Jesus (see 2 Pet 2:4-9). The Old Testament, then, deserves to be read for its own sake. But the Old Testament is also interpreted by what Jesus has accomplished. That is, the Old Testament must also be understood in reference to Jesus Christ. Indeed, in the perspective of the writer of Hebrews, in Jesus we see clearly the truth revealed only in veiled form in the Old Testament. This phenomenon is illustrated by the early church's interpretation of Isaiah 52:13—53:12.

In contemporary studies, this passage from Isaiah is classed with the Servant Songs, and its words are often viewed as an unmistakable reference to Jesus. In New Testament times Jesus was regarded as the Servant of the Lord (for example, Acts 3:13, 26; 1 Pet 2:21-24). Later, the Christian church made even more explicit use of the Servant idea in describing

Jesus. Thus Athanasius, the fourth-century Bishop of Alexandria, wrote of Jesus:

> Nor is even his death passed over in silence; on the contrary it is referred to in the divine Scriptures, even exceeding clearly. For to the end that none should err for want of instruction in the actual events, they feared not to mention even the cause of his death—that he suffers it, not for his own sake, but for the immortality and salvation of all, and the counsels of the Jews against him and the indignities offered him at their hands.[17]

Athanasius goes on to support his assertions with extended quotations from Isaiah 53:3-10, which he calls a "certain reference" to the death of Jesus.

Whatever Athanasius held, Isaiah 52:13—53:12 is not necessarily as clear a reference to the Messiah as we might think. The term *Messiah* never appears in the text, nor is there any mention of the "Son of David." Furthermore, some evidence suggests that the Servant in Isaiah may have been a collective term for Israel, as well as, perhaps, for an individual. It is not insignificant that Jewish speculation about the Messiah did not focus on this text; while it attached the term *Messiah* to other Old Testament concepts and titles, there is little evidence indeed of its having developed any notion of a "Suffering Messiah" from Isaiah 53. Though in denying that Christ can be found anywhere in the Old Testament, von Rad has certainly overstated his case. He is more generally correct when he observes that the Old Testament does not visualize such a man as appears in the Gospels and Epistles.[18] The meaning of the Suffering Servant in relation to the Messiah becomes clear *only* upon reading Isaiah 53 with Jesus' life and work in view. Because there are so many points of comparison between the Servant of the Lord and Jesus, Isaiah 53 has become a text of great import for the Christian church. This is a result, however, of reading Isaiah through the lens provided by the life of Jesus.

How does all of this affect the way we read the Old Testament, especially its prophetic portions, today? First, we again must see that the Old Testament has significance in and of itself. The Old Testament is not simply a launching pad for messianic proof-texts and types of Jesus. Major New Testament themes and theological concepts have their background in the Old Testament, and it will not do to read the New Testament back into the Old to gain insight on these points. Much can be learned by studying the Old Testament passages within their own contexts, for their own sakes.

Second, it is apparent that Jesus and the New Testament writers have left their stamp on the interpretation of the Old Testament prophetic tradition. As we will see in greater detail in the next chapter, prophecy is at times fulfilled in unanticipated ways. At some points, the Old Testament has undergone radical reinterpretation in the light of Jesus' life and work. Thus, it is perfectly legitimate, even necessary, to also interpret the Old Testament through the eyes of the New. In fact, ultimately Old Testament predictions are interpreted in their true perspective only when they are focused on the Messiah of God, Christ Jesus.[19]

8
Prophecy
Fulfilled

"How do the present developments in the Middle East relate to biblical prophecy?" That question awaited me when I
entered a Christian gathering in June 1982. Surprisingly,
Israel, long on the defensive, had suddenly turned aggressor,
flexing its military muscle, thus provoking a new wave of interest in the modern fulfillment of biblical prophecy. Surely—
or so it was thought—the present conflict was somehow described in the prophecy against Gog in Ezekiel 38—39. Hal
Lindsey's claim, "the pages of Ezekiel's and Daniel's prophecies are beginning to look like today's headlines," appeared
to be gaining supportive evidence.[1]

On a superficial level the connection between the conflict
in question and Ezekiel's prophecy could be dismissed easily
enough. In this case Israel was on the offensive, not the helpless victim in the hands of Gog. More basically, attempts to
link that modern situation with this prophecy failed to read
the biblical text in view of its own historical circumstances.[2]
Nevertheless, even erroneous pointers to a modern realization of an ancient prophecy raise an important issue: Some

truly forward-looking prophecies have yet to be fulfilled. Can
we with any precision pinpoint the fulfillment of such prophecies in our own day?

An outstanding example of an eschatological prophecy
awaiting fulfillment is the picture in Revelation 11:15:

> The seventh angel sounded his trumpet, and there were
> loud voices in heaven, which said:
>
> "The kingdom of the world has become the
>   kingdom of our Lord and of his Christ,
> and he will reign for ever and ever."

This passage anticipating the return of Jesus and establish-
ment of his kingdom, along with a myriad of other such passages, has not yet been fulfilled. Scores of additional prophecies might be set forth as awaiting fulfillment; indeed, contemporary interest in the prophetic Scriptures has often
focused entirely on delineating unfulfilled prophecies and
indicating how they will be fulfilled in our own generation.

Persons who explain current events in terms of fulfilled
prophecy, or who gather together so-called unfulfilled prophecies into an end-time schedule, face three major stumbling
blocks: first, the ambiguity associated with the prophetic
word itself; second, the problem of the conditional nature of
prophecy; third, the possibility of unexpected fulfillment of
predictive prophecy. We will discuss each of these three in
turn and then briefly illustrate the problem of mapping out the
future with reference to Jesus' "signs of the times" and the
"antichrist."

Ambiguities in the Prophetic Word

It is not always easy to distinguish present from future-looking elements in the words of the prophets. Already we have
seen that prophecy was more *forth*telling than *fore*telling, and
this distinction can hardly be overemphasized when dealing
with the issue of fulfilled prophecy. The prophets were not
speaking primarily to later generations, but to their own. Yet

the eschatological element does appear from time to time in their oracles. Even then, however, its role is subservient to the central theme the prophets wished to communicate. The prophetic Scriptures are misused when treated as a grab bag of end-time predictions.

Distinguishing present from future-looking elements in the words of the prophets is further complicated because the biblical writers themselves sometimes understand certain biblical texts to refer to both present and future events. One of the clearest examples of this is Moses' statement in Deuteronomy 18:15: "The LORD your God will raise up for you a prophet like me." As we have seen, this passage originally signified that God would speak to his people through a man of God like Moses, and not through some form of pagan sorcery.[3] However, the passage later took on an eschatological meaning and was understood as a promise of a great prophetic mediator—a Messiah, like Moses. Might other passages take on new meanings too? We have noted in the previous chapter that certain texts were applied to the Christ once they were determined to have double meanings. According to R. T. France, "the fact that many of the so-called 'Messianic' prophecies of the Old Testament appear to have a primary reference to the prophet's own historical situation, and express his hope for the near future, does not rule out a further eschatological reference."[4]

There is reason to believe that in many instances a text could have a second, yet-to-be-fulfilled dimension. Words of the prophets, however, are not guaranteed a second, or multiple, reference. Nor are we given any clues for discerning or explaining that possible additional dimension. Therefore, to mine prophetic texts which were not predictive originally, or which have already been fulfilled, in order to find in them a further, unfulfilled, eschatological dimension is to resort to pure, unfounded speculation.

More confusing, the prophets are often inexact when they refer to time and the future. Consider, for example, the

promised return of Christ Jesus. Second Peter 3 deals in part
with those who scoff at that promise because it has not yet
taken place. The author asserts: "Do not forget this one thing,
dear friends: With the Lord a day is like a thousand years, and
a thousand years are like a day. The Lord is not slow in keeping his promise, as some understand slowness" (vv. 8-9).

It is hard to tie down words like *soon* and *short* especially in
light of God's perspective on time. In fact, when the prophets
speak of what will happen, emphasis falls more on the *certainty*
of the event than on the time of its happening.

So far we have not mentioned the key source of ambiguity
in prophecy: symbolic language. We do not need to repeat
what we have already said in chapter six about symbolism.
Symbolic language can be the interpreter's nightmare; yet
even in passages that use no symbolism at all, the attempt to
pinpoint with exactitude the prophetic reference to a future,
unfulfilled event is often a moot exercise. The prophets were
little concerned about the distant future, and we should not
project our own curiosity about what will be onto those of another era who had other legitimate concerns.

Conditional Prophecy

In the previous chapter we saw how tightly the Hebrew people held to the utter faithfulness of God. Among them grew
the conviction that what God had promised he would do—
even if that promise must be projected to the future. Likewise,
in our day, some interpreters assert that those promises and
prophecies not yet literally fulfilled will eventually be realized.
These interpreters argue, for example, that the Abrahamic
covenant gives the Jewish people perpetual title to the land of
Palestine (see Gen 17:8). They hold that this covenant between God and Abraham had no strings attached; thus,
prophecies related to it will be fulfilled in the future. Pentecost states:

This Abrahamic covenant, which contained individual

promises to Abraham, promises of the preservation of a nation, and the possession of a land by that nation, was given to a specific covenant people. Since it was unconditional and eternal, and has never yet been fulfilled, it must await a future fulfillment, Israel must be preserved as a nation, must inherit her land, and be blessed with spiritual blessings to make this inheritance possible.[5]

This line of argument will not stand close scrutiny. Contrary to what some would have us believe, the Abrahamic covenant was not unconditional. Otherwise, why would God have said to Abraham, "As for you, you must keep my covenant, you and your descendants after you" (Gen 17:9)? First God says what he will do ("As for me, . . . " vv. 1-8); then he outlines what Abraham must do ("As for you, . . . " vv. 9-14) to keep the covenant. On one level, circumcision is the required act; in fact, an uncircumcised male was cut off from his people as a covenant breaker (v. 14). Yet circumcision was only a "sign of the covenant" (v. 11). More fundamentally, God demanded obedience of Abraham and his offspring in receiving and keeping his gracious offer. Elsewhere it was also made clear that the promise of the land was conditional, based on continuing obedience:

Genesis 18:16-19—God has chosen Abraham so that Abraham will bring up his family to obey the Lord, so that the Lord will do what he has promised.
Genesis 22:15-18—Because of Abraham's obedience he and his descendants will receive God's blessing.
Genesis 26:2-5—Because of Abraham's obedience, his descendants through Isaac will receive the lands.
Leviticus 26:27-33—If Israel is disobedient the land will be wasted, inhabited by enemies; Israel will be scattered. Disobedience will lead to denial of all of the hopes enshrined in the Abrahamic covenant.[6]

The promise of the land was conditional, and because of disobedience Israel was time and time again separated from that

land. "The fulfillment of God's marvelous promises, including the promise of the land, hinged upon Israel's fidelity."[7]
(See Deuteronomy 7:12-15.) Later, in the seventh century
B.C., Jeremiah proclaimed the word of the Lord: "Reform
your ways and your actions, and I will let you live in this place"
(7:3; see also vv. 5-7).

Has Israel's disobedience led to God's declaring this covenant (with the promise of perpetual ownership of the land)
null and void? In a moment we will see that, despite the fail-
ures of his people, God has graciously upheld his end of the
contract—*but in a surprising way.*

Predictive prophecy is by nature conditional. To call for
an eventual literal fulfillment of every unfulfilled word is to
misunderstand the nature of prophecy and the character of
God. Biblical prophecy is not some statement of fate which
must see its end no matter what. We have seen that the prophets sometimes used statements about the future in order to
bring about change in the present; now, we may also note that
the people's response to prophecy played a consequential
role in determining how the prophetic words were realized.
Jonah prophesied, "Forty more days and Nineveh will be
destroyed." But forty days, and more, passed without the
promised destruction. Why? The Ninevites had turned to
God in faith and repentance. "When God saw what they did
and how they turned from their evil ways, he had compassion
and did not bring upon them the destruction he had threatened" (Jon 3:10).

As Jonah's story well illustrates, God can change his mind.
Jeremiah, too, relates God's capacity to alter his own prescrip-
tions whenever he wills.

If at any time I announce that a nation or kingdom is to be
uprooted, torn down and destroyed, and if that nation I
warned repents of its evil, then I will relent and not inflict
on it the disaster I had planned. And if at another time I
announce that a nation or kingdom is to be built up and

planted, and if it does evil in my sight and does not obey
me, then I will reconsider the good I had intended to do
for it. (Jer 18:7-10)
This statement of principle is aimed at Israel (18:6). It clearly signifies that Israel will receive God's gracious favor only
if Israel obeys the covenant. Moreover, this passage shows
that the initiative for blessing and destruction, and for promise and fulfillment, lies always with God. He is not bound
by some sort of prophetic inertia to bless a disobedient people.

The conditional nature of prophecy, when taken seriously,
raises serious questions about the usefulness of outlining what
must or must not happen before the end. The study of biblical prophecy puts no one one-up on God, as if his every move
were known beforehand. Because of human infidelity, some
promises may have been nullified or amended. The preroga-
tive to determine what lies ahead is always God's.

Unexpected Fulfillment

Finally, the interpreter who wants to pinpoint modern fulfillment of biblical prophecy must face the reality that the fulfillment is often not quite what was anticipated. Not only do
some prophetic passages acquire new meaning with time, as
we saw earlier, but the realization of a prophecy often contains an element of surprise, frequently going far beyond the
original prediction.[8] Jesus himself is the best illustration of a
surprising fulfillment. It is sometimes asked, How could the
Jewish experts on the Old Testament have failed to recognize
Jesus as the promised Messiah? After all, they more than anyone else would have been aware of the characteristics of God's
Chosen One. The answer is simple enough: "There is no com-
pelling way from prophecy (i.e., the Old Testament) to the
fulfillment in [Jesus] Christ."[9] Study of the Old Testament
did not prepare the Jews for a crucified Messiah; indeed, the
cross of Christ was a stumbling block for Jews (1 Cor 1:23).
Expecting a literal fulfillment of their hope for a political Mes-

siah who would deliver them from bondage and oppression, they were unable to grasp the divine significance of Jesus' work. Only with hindsight could Jesus' relationship to the Old Testament prophecies be readily seen as fulfillment of promise.

When fulfillment exceeds promise, three things are underscored: God's freedom and creativity and the historical quality of biblical prophecy. Given in particular, historical circumstances, prophecy uses words and ideas appropriate to its day. A different historical situation at the time of fulfillment, however, may involve a realization in updated terms beyond the literal meaning of the original prediction. Stephen Travis offers this illustration:

> A little girl looks forward to Christmas and to the present which her parents have promised to give her. A doll that walks is what she has her heart on. Christmas Day arrives, and what is waiting at the bottom of her bed? A doll that not only walks but talks and weeps and wets her nappy! The little girl did not even know such things had been invented, but she does not dream of complaining that she was not given what she hoped for. Of course not. She is thrilled with the ability of mum and dad to come up with surprises which more than fulfill her expectations.[10]

The promise to Abraham of a land, discussed earlier, provides an eye-opening biblical example of this idea. In the Old Testament, the land was considered God's to give as he willed; moreover, to dwell in the land was to enjoy the gracious presence of God. The promised land was the "inheritance" (see Ps 68:9-10; 79:1; 105:11; Jer 2:7). In the New Testament Abraham's inheritance, the promised land, took the form of "a better country—a heavenly one" (Heb 11:8-16). Indeed, the Old Testament concept of the inheritance was recast in the New to designate the all-embracing concept of the kingdom of God (see Mt 19:29; 1 Cor 15:50; Tit 3:7; Heb 6:12-13; 1 Pet 1:3-4; Rev 21:7).[11] The promise of the land

awaits complete fulfillment in a new form, that of the believers' heavenly dwelling with God.

If we acknowledge that ancient prophecies may be fulfilled in ways we do not expect, it follows that we cannot
employ prophecies as detailed blueprints of the future. We
may see general parallels between the prophet's situation
and our own; however, we must leave room for unforeseen
variations.

Signs of the Times

Two popular themes in current discussions of biblical prophecy highlight the problems of neatly packaged biblical predictions. First, we will look at the "signs of the times" or "signs
of the end of the age" found in Mark 13 (compare Mt 24). The
scene opens when Jesus, after the disciples have declared the
splendor of the temple buildings, says that these buildings
will be destroyed. Later, a small group of disciples asks him,
"Tell us, when will these things happen? And what will be the
sign that they are all about to be fulfilled?" (v. 4). This question concerned not only the destruction of the temple, but
also the end of the world.[12] As for *when*, in verse 32 Jesus
dismisses that question as inappropriate. In response to the
disciples' question about what sign, or indicator, in the present
would point to the coming end, Jesus relates not a sign (singu-
lar), but a whole list of signs—signs ambiguous because of
their universality!

A key to interpreting these signs is given in Mark 13:8:
"These are the beginning of birth pains." Hal Lindsey notes
the importance of this phrase, but interprets it erroneously.
He suggests that we understand "birth pains" as we understand the term today. He writes:

> I saw the image of the nervous first-time father anxiously
> timing the space between his wife's painful contractions to
> determine the nearness of birth. The pain itself is not his
> signal: Only when the pains become more frequent and

more intense does he know that the baby is about to be born.[13]

Lindsey concludes, then, that as the signs listed by Jesus become more frequent and intense, the end draws nearer. He observes that the appearance of these signs has accelerated in the last ten years, which suggests to him that the end is just around the corner.

The problem with Lindsey's interpretation is that he reads a twentieth-century understanding of "birth pains" back into the first century. The real question for us is, What meaning was attached to "birth pains" in New Testament times? For example, Paul uses the word in 1 Thessalonians 5:3 to signify the suddenness of an event: "Destruction will come on them suddenly, as labor pains on a pregnant woman, and they will not escape." There is no thought of increasing frequency or intensity here. Or, in Galatians 4:19, Paul speaks of his own "pains of childbirth" to vividly express his acute love and concern for the Christians at Galatia. Mark 13:8 presents us with a different usage, particularly since here we encounter apocalyptic thought not unlike that found in Romans 8:22: "The whole creation has been groaning as in the pains of childbirth right up to the present time." "Birth pains," in fact, had already at the time of Jesus become a technical metaphor in apocalyptic thought for the birth of God's people into the eschaton.[14]

To describe these signs as the beginning of birth pains, then, has a dual significance. On the one hand, these signs are physical, earthly manifestations of the heavenly war being carried out as God brings in the new age, the consummated kingdom of God. They indicate that the ultimate time of salvation is near. On the other hand, the reference to "the beginning of birth pains" indicates that the gestation period is not completed. One should not be overhasty in expecting the end. Jesus does not outline the signs to enable us to work out God's end-time schedule. Mark 13:7 makes explicit that even when these signs occur, as they must, the end is still to come. Hence, these signs do not refer exclusively to the time just before the end. Moreover, as a reading of Mark 13 will show, these signs are not at all spectacular; each of them has been visible at every period in the history of the church![15]

From the signs of the end given by Jesus, we are unable to construct an exact time-line leading up to the end, nor can we calculate the time of the end itself. All we can say is that we live in the end times, just as every Christian generation has.

The Antichrist

A second popular theme showing the hazards of trying to find prophecy fulfilled in the modern era concerns the "antichrist."[16] This figure is described primarily in the letters of John, 2 Thessalonians and Revelation, though additional hints or traces of this figure may be located elsewhere.

The actual word *antichrist* appears only in 1 and 2 John, where the antichrist—or better, antichrists—are theological figures. The readers of 1 John were already familiar with the antichrist, for his coming had been prophesied (1 Jn 2:18; 4:3). Now antichrists were present in their community; they were deceivers, false teachers, from among the members of the church (1 Jn 2:19); they denied the Father and the Son (1 Jn 2:22) and refused to acknowledge the incarnation of Jesus Christ (2 Jn 7). We note in these references a certain ambivalence: Are we reading of one figure yet to come, a prophecy of one figure fulfilled by the coming of many, or the appearance of both antichrists and the antichrist? Probably the author regards the false teachers of his day as antichrists—possessed by the spirit of antichrist (1 Jn 4:3)—but leaves open the possibility of a future antichrist as well.

Revelation never mentions the antichrist by name, but gives a picture of the figure in chapter thirteen as the personification of the evil power opposed to God. Revelation 13 portrays "the beast from the sea" as the counterimage of the Savior of the world. This is a political antichrist, the Roman emperor demanding divine adoration. In claiming for himself the title *Lord* the emperor became for Christians a rival Christ, an antichrist.

Finally, 2 Thessalonians 2:3-4 speaks of the revealing of "the man of lawlessness" who will lead a great rebellion before the coming of the Day of the Lord. This man exalts himself as if he were God, and opposes all that is God's.[17] He is the very embodiment of lawlessness, the ultimate opponent against God.

These important texts are linked together by their descriptions of the antichrist; however, it is not possible to draw from these passages any comprehensive description incorporating all the various pieces. Only by speaking in broad generalizations can one refer to *the* New Testament teaching on the antichrist. Because the antichrist appears in various forms in the New Testament, Gordon D. Fee asks a highly relevant question: "How are *we* to understand this figure with regard to our own future?"[18] What we can know with certainty is that whoever the antichrist was, is or will be, he is "doomed to destruction" (2 Thess 2:3; Rev 19:20; 1 Jn 4:4).

The consummation of the kingdom of God, the ushering in of the new age lies before us. About the fullness of that kingdom, swept to the fore by the return of Jesus, we can be certain. We have seen in this chapter, however, the uselessness of trying to predict when the eschaton will be realized. Attempts at scheduling this or that event, or even at discerning which pre-end-time event ought to be scheduled, have no firm basis in the Scriptures. The Bible simply offers little that will help us find in our own era the certain fulfillment of prophesied events. The signs are not clear: the end is ever near—perhaps today, perhaps not. We must reject the way of inconclusive speculation and embrace the way of longing for, and proclaiming, the coming kingdom.

9
Prophecy and God's Purpose

The whole Bible, and not only its prophetic and apocalyptic sections, is concerned with "the last things."[1] This is particularly clear in the New Testament, where the destiny of history —and with history all of creation—is at center stage. The Old Testament, too, is not without explicit witness to the future. Already in its third chapter a pointer to the messianic age arises (Gen 3:15). The Bible, however, need not speak in the future tense or use phrases like "the last days" to show the interrelation of its message with what is to come. Christians affirm the continuity of the present with the past and future. We believe in a Lord who is "the Alpha and the Omega, the First and the Last, the Beginning and the End" (Rev 22:13). Thus our understanding of the prophetic and apocalyptic Scriptures is inseparable from our approach to the whole Bible and its witness to God's eternal purpose. That is, our interpretation of the prophetic and apocalyptic canonical writings must take seriously what God has been doing from creation onward.

In this chapter we will briefly survey God's overarching plan. Along the way, several important concepts for the biblical writers will come into view—the kingdom of God, the last days, the Second Coming and others. Finally, we will point out several significant implications for interpreting prophecy.

God's Purpose in Creation

Probably the most significant lesson in the Bible's first two chapters, the creation story, concerns the relation between God and his creation. According to the Genesis account, everything that exists comes from God (compare Rom 11:36; 1 Cor 8:6). Human beings, on the one hand, are very much at one with all other animals—they are brought forth from the ground (Gen 1:24; 2:7). Yet the human is set apart from all other creatures in that the human is made in God's own image (Gen 1:26). In the human, God created a true counterpart, a covenant partner unto himself. Hence, the human has the capacity—and the calling—to enter into and live in close relationship with God. The relational nature of man and woman extends further to include all other humans and, indeed, all of creation. As bearers of the divine image, man and woman at creation had the ability to relate as God relates.[2] In this way, from the very outset, within the order of creation itself, God provided for communion between himself and humanity.

For such communion to be meaningful the human was given the ability to respond freely to God, to return that love first given by God. With the capacity to turn to God in love, fellowship and worship, however, came the option to refuse the God-given call, to reject communion with God.

While man's highest calling was to serve God, he was unique in being the only creature who could respond to God in obedience as well as disobedience, in faith and trust as well as in rebellion and distrust. Unlike the animal creation, which obeys on the basis of instinctive impulses and laws, man and woman were given the freedom of will as part of their mental and spiritual heritage. Man and woman were given the possibility of separating themselves from God just as easily as they could maintain fellowship with Him.[3] God's purpose in creation, while encompassing all that he had made, centered on communion with humanity. However, in allowing rather than forcing persons to respond to him in love and adoration, God left open the possibility of his purpose being frustrated. Humanity might not choose communion with God.

In fact, man and woman rejected God's purpose, as the story of the Fall demonstrates (Gen 3). Asserting themselves against God, they tried to become like God, thus denying their creaturely status, their utter dependence on God (Gen 3:1-6). The result was, and is, alienation from God (Gen 3: 7-10, 22-24), from other humans (3:12-13) and from all nonhuman creation (3:17-19). This tale is an important chapter in the history of a cosmic conflict—good versus evil, light versus darkness, God versus Satan—which even now rushes toward the end.

The Two Kingdoms

The Bible speaks of this conflict in terms of two kingdoms. One is known as the kingdom of God; the other is called by various names: the kingdom of the world, the kingdom of darkness or the kingdom of Satan, to name only three. Once, when accused by the Pharisees of operating by the power of Beelzebub, Jesus placed these two kingdoms in stark contrast:

> Every kingdom divided against itself will be ruined. . . . If Satan drives out Satan, he is divided against himself. How then can his kingdom stand? And if I drive out demons by Beelzebub, by whom do your people drive them out? . . . But if I drive out demons by the Spirit of God, then the kingdom of God has come upon you. (Mt 12:25-28)

The introduction of a kingdom that opposes God ruptures God's order of creation.[4]

Ruled by "the god of this age" (2 Cor 4:4; compare with Mt
4:8), the kingdom of darkness is hostile toward God. Conflict
on a grand scale is at work, for "the whole world is under the
control of the evil one" (1 Jn 5:19). As Christians, we are called
to arm ourselves against "the powers of this dark world and
against the spiritual forces of evil in the heavenly realms" (Eph
6:12). Even though Satan may rule in this world, the creation
is still God's. Ultimately, the kingdom of darkness will not
have its way. Proclaimed in both Old and New Testaments is
the final, complete victory of God's kingdom over all opposing
forces.

Although the phrase *kingdom of God* is absent from the Old
Testament, the concept itself is present—first in the notion of
God as king, then in expressions related to his coming reign.[5]
The Old Testament gives expression to God's kingship over
the world in general (for example, Ps 29:10; 47:2; 96:10; Is
6:5; Jer 46:18), and over Israel in particular (for example, Ex
15:18; Deut 33:5; Is 43:15). First and foremost, God's kingdom meant his active reign, his sovereign rule, and not a
physical or material realm. The hope centered on the coming
kingdom of God had to do with his authority, rule and justice.

Let the sea resound, and all that is in it,
    the world, and all who live in it.
Let the rivers clap their hands,
    let the mountains sing together for joy;
let them sing before the LORD,
    for he comes to judge the earth.
He will judge the world in righteousness
    and the peoples with equity. (Ps 98:7-9)

Here all creation rejoices when men and women are again
under the reign of their God.

It is that rule, God's kingdom over the whole world, that is
anticipated by the classical Old Testament prophets and by
Daniel, as in this passage from Zechariah: "The LORD will be
king over the whole earth. On that day there will be one LORD,

and his name the only name" (14:9).

Isaiah, too, proclaims the coming kingdom of God—a time of renewed communion and peace among all peoples, all under the reign of God:

He will judge between the nations
  and will settle disputes for many peoples.
They will beat their swords into plowshares
  and their spears into pruning hooks.
Nation will not take up sword against nation,
  nor will they train for war anymore. (2:4)

In Daniel the kingdom set up by God will destroy all other kingdoms, "but it will itself endure forever" (2:44; compare with Ps 45:5-6). It is said in Daniel 7:13-14 that God's reign will be in the hands of "one like a son of man" and will include all peoples. "His dominion is an everlasting dominion that will not pass away, and his kingdom is one that will never be destroyed" (7:14).

The New Testament begins with a proclamation of the kingdom's nearness.[6] "In those days John the Baptist came, preaching in the Desert of Judea and saying, 'Repent, for the kingdom of heaven is near' " (Mt 3:1). In this saying and elsewhere in Matthew where the expression *kingdom of heaven* appears, *heaven* does not designate the location of the kingdom, but its source. *Heaven* is a substitute word for God here, a not uncommon usage in pre-Christian Judaism. These verses record how John prophesied the coming fulfillment of Israel's hope and urged his audiences to prepare accordingly, through repentance and baptism. As we saw in chapter seven, Israel's expectations often centered on God's agent of salvation, the one through whom he would bring his promises to fruition. John announced the fulfillment of that expectation through one who would pronounce judgment and bestow the gift of the Holy Spirit (Mt 3:11-12).

The first summary of Jesus' preaching in Mark reveals similarity between his message and John's: "After John was delivered up, Jesus came into Galilee, proclaiming the good news of God, and saying, 'The time has been fulfilled; the kingdom of God is near. Repent and believe the good news!' " (Mk 1:14-15). Yet however much alike, the messages of John and Jesus are marked by a far-reaching distinction. Jesus, unlike John, announced the fulfillment of time; for Jesus the reign of God was not simply near, it had invaded history! In Jesus' coming, the kingdom had come (see Mt 12:28; 13:44-46; Lk 17:20-21). Throughout his teaching ministry the kingdom of God was ever on Jesus' lips. He taught its present realization—especially through parables—and his actions confirmed his verbal message. On every hand he anticipated the conquest of evil. He forgave sins on his own authority. He drove out demons. He healed the sick. He even raised the dead. It is no wonder, then, that the people "were all filled with awe" and said, "God has visited his people" (Lk 7:16). They were confident that they were witnessing the fulfillment of God's promised salvation.[7]

The early church was equally confident that God's reign had begun in Jesus' first coming. In one of the rare New Testament occurrences of *kingdom* outside the Gospels, Paul links the presence of the kingdom with God's promised salvation and declares its triumph over the kingdom of Satan: "For [God] has rescued us from the dominion of darkness and brought us into the kingdom of the Son he loves, in whom we have redemption, the forgiveness of sins" (Col 1:13-14). Paul also speaks of the kingdom of God in the ethical discussion of Romans 14:17. In addition to employing the phrase *kingdom of God,* the New Testament has other ways of proclaiming God's present reign. Most notably, to confess "Jesus is Lord" is to proclaim the presence of God's kingdom (see Acts 8:12; 28:31).

The Present and the Not Yet
For Jesus, and for the early church, the kingdom of God had

come into the world at Jesus' first coming; for them the kingdom is present. Yet in another sense the kingdom is "not
yet." As Howard Marshall writes:

> The new era promised in the Old Testament had in fact
> arrived. It did not, however, mean that the old era came to
> an end. The gospel message was not universally received,
> and sin and death continued to hold sway.[8]

The tension between the *present* and the *not yet* is found in
Jesus' teaching. We have already spoken of Jesus' proclamation of the presence of the kingdom; he also speaks of the
kingdom as awaiting fulfillment: for example, in the Sermon
on the Mount (Mt 7:21-23), in the parable of the wedding
banquet (Mt 22:1-14) and in the parable of the weeds (Mt
13:24-30, 36-43). Matthew 25:1-13, the parable of the ten vir-
gins, also paints an eschatological portrait of the kingdom.

Apostolic Christianity, as we know it from the New Testament, likewise spoke of the coming reign of God. The early
Christian hymn recorded in Philippians 2:6-11 witnesses to
the future consummation of God's purpose, when

> at the name of Jesus every knee shall bow
>   in heaven and on earth and under the earth,
> and every tongue confess that Jesus Christ is Lord,
>   to the glory of God the Father. (vv. 10-11)

Second Timothy 4:18 testifies to the author's conviction that
the Lord "will bring me safely to his heavenly kingdom." This
two-edged affirmation about God's reign is well represented
in the title of George Eldon Ladd's book on the kingdom, *The
Presence of the Future.* By way of summary, we can do little better than to affirm his central thesis

that the Kingdom of God is the redemptive reign of God
dynamically active to establish his rule among men, and
that this Kingdom, which will appear as an apocalyptic act
at the end of the age, has already come into human history
in the person and mission of Jesus to overcome evil, to deliver men from its power, and to bring them into the bless-

ings of God's reign.[9]
Hence, the fulfillment of time occurred with the advent of
Jesus (Mk 1:15; Gal 4:4), but the consummation of the
kingdom is a future event (see Rev 21:1-4).

This present epoch, then, is a time of transition. The old
age has come under divine judgment and is doomed to end.
The new age, God's kingdom, is present for those "with eyes
to see and ears to hear." According to the author of Hebrews,
we live in a city which will not endure, "but we are looking for
the city that is to come" (13:14). We live in the last period of
human history before God restores everything, "as he promised long ago through his holy prophets" (Acts 3:21).

Did the Old Testament prophets foresee this present era?
After the outpouring of the Holy Spirit at Pentecost, Peter
explained that this was what was spoken by the prophet Joel
when he described the last days (Acts 2:16). The writer of Hebrews also marks this present period as the last days (1:1-2;
compare with 9:26). Thus interpreters who insist that the
Hebrew prophets failed to see this "age of grace," the "church
age," themselves fail to take seriously the apostolic testimony.[10]
Moreover, any who proclaim these days as the last days because of apparent impending doom on economic, military or
ecological fronts have missed the biblical point entirely.[11] The
pointed message of the New Testament is that the last days
were initiated with the resurrection of the crucified Christ
and the outpouring of the Holy Spirit, and that these last days
will continue until the Second Coming of Jesus. These in-
terim days are days for repentance, faith and widespread loyalty to Christ—a time of mission, of being about the work of
the kingdom. These last days are days of anticipating, working toward and hoping for the last day, the Day of the Lord.

Israel and the Kingdom
What, then, of Israel? What is the relation between Israel
and kingdom? Some in our day hold that because Israel re-

jected Jesus, the offer of the kingdom was postponed until
Jesus' Second Coming, at which time all of God's eternal covenants with Israel will be fulfilled. Hence, the kingdom is not
yet, and it is tied to Israel.[12] Equally dogmatic are those who
argue that the promises given to Israel have been, are being
and will be fulfilled in and through the new people of God,
the church of Jesus Christ. The issues involved are many, and
some are complex. Israel is not the focus of our discussion;
hence, we will consider only a few programmatic points.

1. We have seen the necessity of interpreting the Old Testament in light of the New. Therefore, whatever decision we
reach must deal adequately with the New Testament evidence.

2. The coming kingdom of God is the consummation of
God's eternal purpose in creation. This purpose includes, but
transcends, the people of Israel.

3. Moreover, the kingdom of God is not only a future entity.
The kingdom is God's reign, already begun. One should not
then, draw too straight a line from Israel to kingdom of God.

4. In the Old Testament, Israel was known as the people of
God: in Hebrew, *qahal;* in Greek, *ekklesia.*[13] It is of no little
consequence that the early church took over for themselves
the Old Testament designation for Israel—the *ekklesia* of God.
In this same vein, Paul seems to equate true Israel with Christians, whether Jews or Gentiles (see Rom 2:25, 28-29; Gal 3:7;
Phil 3:3)—an equation made more clearly in 1 Peter 2:9-10,
echoing the language of Israel's election in Exodus 19:6.

5. The New Testament relates Old Testament prophecies
concerning Israel to the church. Jeremiah 31:31, for instance,
tells how God will make a new covenant with *Israel.* This new
covenant is said in the New Testament to be a covenant in
Jesus' blood (Lk 22:20; 1 Cor 11:25; Heb 7—8)—a covenant
given the church.

6. In the New Testament, old distinctions between Jews and
Gentiles (regarding their standing before God) break down.
See Acts 10:1—11:18; Galatians 3:26-29; Ephesians 2:11-19.

7. God's purpose in his initial election of Israel was not that Israel might receive a special blessing from God, but that Israel might have a special position of servanthood. Israel was to serve among the nations as priests (Ex 19:6; compare with Gen 12:3)—"a guide for the blind, a light for those who are in the dark, an instructor of the foolish, a teacher of infants" (Rom 2:19-20). But Israel neglected the vocation given by God (Rom 2:17-24; compare with Acts 13:46-48). Now God's mission in the world is the task of the church.

8. Some verses would appear to settle the issue of God's purpose for Israel with great ease. Some consider Romans 11:26—"And so all Israel will be saved"—to be unequivocal proof of God's continuing and future purpose for Israel. On the other hand, Paul's apparent reference to the Christian church as "the Israel of God" (Gal 6:16) seems a certain witness to the idea that the church has superseded Israel in God's plan. However, caution must be exercised here. Both texts, and others like them, are full of exegetical entanglements. In considering such texts as evidence for the problem of Israel one must be careful to relate them to all other relevant texts as well as to the general force of New Testament theology.

The Church and the Kingdom

More pertinent to our discussion is the relation of the church to God's kingdom.[14] In a superficial sense, it is possible to identify the church with God's kingdom: the Lord's present reign is most visible in the church. Nonetheless, it must be stated emphatically: the church is *not* the kingdom.[15] The kingdom is the universal, final, eternal, perfect, transcendent and definitive reign of God. The church is none of these! Although its members are reconciled to God in Christ, the church is imperfect, made up of sinners. Moreover, the church is provisional, not eternal; it will pass away when that which is perfect has come. The power and glory of God's reign are "not yet."

It is not the Church but the consummated reign of God
which is reflected in so many parables: those of the tree
overshadowing the earth, of the rich harvest, of the feast
given by God, of the eschatological marriage feast. It is not
the Church but the consummated reign of God which is the
goal of creation: the new creation, in which the distinctions
between Church and world will be ovecome.[16]

Yet a strict division between church and kingdom might prove
misleading, for the kingdom of God is inseparable from God's
redemptive activity in history, in which the church plays an
important part. Furthermore, the church anticipates and
signifies the kingdom; it exists "for God, for the Creator and
Lord of the world, for the fulfillment of His purpose and will
for all humanity and the world."[17] In carrying out its mission
the church announces through word and deed that "the kingdom of God is at hand." In proclaiming Jesus as Lord the
church calls the world to repentance and faith in view of God's
present, and coming, reign. The church's task, then, is to
serve the present and future reign of God.

When will the kingdom be consummated and God's purpose from creation be fulfilled? At his Second Coming, Christ
Jesus will come in triumph to initiate the new age, bring an
end to time, and show the meaning of history. Jesus' Second
Coming will inaugurate the age of final redemption: Christ
"will appear a second time, not to bear sin, but to bring salvation to those who are waiting for him" (Heb 9:28). The Second
Coming ushers in the kingdom of God in two events: the general resurrection and the judgment.

For Christians the resurrection is a New Testament promise
which gains its meaning and purpose from the resurrection
of Christ Jesus (1 Cor 15). The final resurrection will be
general—that is, it will include those who have responded to
Christ in faith and those who have not. Those still alive will
also be brought into God's presence (see 1 Cor 15:23, 51-52;
1 Thess 4:14-17). In addition, all creation will be transfigured

(see Mt 19:28; Rom 8:20-21).

Christ's return also fulfills the Old Testament anticipation of "the Day of the Lord"—a day of judgment.

> "Surely the day is coming; it will burn like a furnace. All the arrogant and every evildoer will be stubble, and that day that is coming will set them on fire," says the LORD Almighty. "Not a root or a branch will be left to them. But for you who revere my name, the sun of righteousness will rise with healing in its wings. And you will go out and leap like calves released from the stall. Then you will trample down the wicked; they will be ashes under the soles of your feet on the day when I do these things," says the LORD Almighty. (Mal 4:1-3)

The Second Coming will spell the ultimate triumph of God's reign over all forms of opposition to his eternal purpose. Evil, and all who have followed its way, will come under divine judgment. On that day God's purpose will be vindicated and all who have followed him faithfully will be given a new existence—the life originally willed for them by the Creator, life in communion with himself. The Day of the Lord marks the fulfillment of God's purpose, for then all creation will be "together under one head, even Christ" (Eph 1:10).

Biblical Prophecy in the Light of the Kingdom

From this brief study of the meaning of the kingdom of God, we can draw a few conclusions that will help us to interpret the prophetic and apocalyptic Scriptures.

1. God's purpose is one. In creation God intended to participate in fellowship with his people—all humanity. In redemption God reconciled men and women to himself in order to put an end to the alienation caused by sin. The consummation will be God's ultimate affirmation of his purpose in creation—eternal communion between himself and his faithful. Heaven will be nothing more than "the life originally willed for us by God the Creator, lived for us by his Son Jesus, and worked in us by his Spirit."[18] God's creative order will be seen further in his ultimate affirmation of human freedom: choosing sin results in alienation from God; continually rejecting God's grace in Christ secures eternal alienation from God. The prophetic and apocalyptic portions of God's Word (as with all the Bible) are best viewed through the lens of God's overarching purpose.

2. *God's purpose is universal in scope.* In these last days, God's favor does not rest in special portion on any particular nation or ethnic group. Rather, God's purpose embraces all people—indeed, all creation. To single out the United States as the "promised land," or Israel as in some special way God's people, is to neglect the all-encompassing purpose of God in creation and redemption, now being worked out.

3. *God's kingdom is God's.* We cannot build the kingdom. We cannot bring the kingdom. We cannot will the kingdom's coming. The kingdom is not a product of human effort, power or will. The kingdom is not the utopian goal of an evolutionary process. The kingdom is God's.

So radical is evil that it will finally be put away only at the consummation of God's kingdom.

We can serve the kingdom. We can prepare for the kingdom. We can pray, "Thy kingdom come." But the kingdom of God will come only through God's power and because he wills it. We will not usher in God's reign.

4. *The present age is an age of tension.* The new has broken in, but the old persists. Thus we find ourselves torn between two kingdoms. The here-and-now message of the prophetic and apocalyptic Scriptures is then especially important to grasp. The present relevance of these Scriptures is highlighted for us. "Remember whose you are." "Declare your loyalty." "No matter how circumstances appear, God is faithful and will triumph."

Living in these in-between times, we are called to faithfulness and service. Our task is to be God's instruments in extending the influence of the kingdom now present in the world

10
The Prophetic Message

Not to tickle our ears with fanciful jargon . . . not to provide raw material for end-time speculation . . . not to prove a stumbling block for Bible interpreters . . . but to fulfill a redemptive and ethical purpose were the prophetic and apocalyptic Scriptures written. It is important for us as Christians then to bend our minds and hearts to their message. Our quest is to apprehend that message and live in it.

In the preceding pages we have observed many obstacles to understanding those parts of the Bible—Ezekiel, Revelation, Amos and the rest—which sometimes appear confusing, even nonsensical. We have outlined a number of principles by which to move beyond those hurdles. Unfortunately—or so it may appear to some—we have not found it possible to present a step-by-step, work-every-time formula in which to plug the biblical texts for immediate and easy comprehension. But we have pointed out some guidelines—keys to the map—which should help the Bible student make sense of biblical prophecy and apocalyptic. In this closing chapter we now need to look further into the question of what these sections of Scripture have to offer. What do we learn from these particular biblical writers? With what challenge do they present us and our world?

Obviously, in one small chapter we cannot follow this line of questioning in any great detail. Indeed, to do so we would have to steal the thunder of the biblical writers themselves! What we can do is develop a few of the more prominent and important points shared by the prophets and apocalyptic writers. This we will do under two headings—the one centering on our *perspective* as Christians, the other on our *motivation*.

Seeing in the Light of God's Ultimate Purpose

How long, O LORD, must I call for help,
    but you do not listen?
Or cry out to you, "Violence!"
    but you do not save?

Why do you make me look at injustice?
    Why do you tolerate wrong?
Destruction and violence are before me;
    there is strife, and conflict abounds.

Therefore the law is paralyzed,
    and justice never prevails.
The wicked hem in the righteous,
    so that justice is perverted. (Hab 1:2-4)

Habakkuk's complaint to the Lord gives us a window into the world of the great prophets. In his anger he typifies the atmosphere of his day; he verbalizes the despairing confusion of a people who have apparently been forgotten by their almighty, just and loving God. God's people, supposed recipients of divine blessing, were suffering at the hands of oppressors. The governing order promoted inequity. Life was unfair. And God was apparently helpless to intervene and set things right. Circumstances made a mockery of God's providence.

An echo of this same ambivalence is heard in the early Christian era on the lips of martyred saints: "How long, Sovereign Lord, holy and true, until you judge the inhabitants of the earth and avenge our blood?" (Rev 6:10). By describing the Lord as they do—"sovereign," "holy" and "true"— they showed their continued faith in God and his capacity to vindicate the cause for which they gave their lives. But their deaths nonetheless raised questions about God's power to intervene on behalf of his own and the truth of the cause of Christ. Their plea was for the Lord to vindicate his name and his work, to show that he was indeed Lord of all and that they were truly his servants.

Why do the righteous suffer? How can a just and loving God permit grave manifestations of evil? These questions persist in our own day. Indeed, such issues may have become even more pressing. On the one hand, we are more and more confronted with the gross injustices of our own world. The plight of our own poor and oppressed is paraded before us by numerous media. Modern day "prophets" will not allow us to turn a deaf ear to the cries of harassed and helpless peoples, nor will they let us forget God's concern for justice and reconciliation.[1] On the other hand, we live in the age of promise, of the outpouring of the Holy Spirit, of the inbreaking kingdom of God. If the cross and resurrection of Jesus really won the decisive victory over evil, then why is this victory not fully evident now? Why does evil abound? Why do the systems of our world continue to operate at cross-purposes with the ways of the sovereign Lord? Why are Christians ridiculed and persecuted? Where is the realization of God's order? How can it be that God is mocked? How long, O Lord? How long before you vindicate your name, your purpose, your people?

The prophetic and apocalyptic Scriptures speak a clear and powerful word concerning the ambiguities and injustices of this world. Their message can open our eyes to a new way of seeing. We can outline some important tenets of this fresh world view:[2]

1. These Scriptures tell us that God is still at work. Like Habakkuk and Elisha's servant (2 Kings 6), we cannot always trust our senses to reveal the whole truth. Even miraculous events, such as those which marked Jesus' ministry, were not always seen as evidence of God's hand at work. The effects of the outpouring of the Holy Spirit at Pentecost were perceived by some as drunken and disorderly conduct (Acts 2:13).

The prophets and apocalyptic writers call us to deeper perceptions, to an openness toward the divine dimension in affairs of this world. They challenge us never to be satisfied with statements about what is until we also account for what God is doing. They appeal to us to view our world through the eyes of faith, that we might know and affirm that God is still at work.

2. These spokesmen for God also tell us that he is ever revealing his eschatological purpose for all the world: a new creation. God is at work in the world establishing his kingdom through Jesus Christ. We can see evidence all about us that God's new creation is invading, passing judgment on and redeeming the old order. Already we are experiencing a foretaste of the riches of the new age.

3. But, the prophets tell us, the fullness of God's redemptive activity does not belong to the present age, but to the age which is to come. It is at Jesus' return that God will "restore everything, as he promised long ago" (Acts 3:21). So the present order is by no means final, nor is it the sphere in which the world will enjoy complete liberation from the cancerous grip of evil and sin.

4. Hence, as we suggested in the preceding chapter, these

days are lived in tension—a reflection of the conflict between God's kingdom and the kingdom of this world. Like the Christians at Corinth, we would be foolish to imagine that we now live in the new age (1 Cor 4:8; compare with Rev 3:17). This, still, is the world of temptation and suffering and death, even if there is also hope and resurrection. The ambiguities of this age are well expressed by Charles Durham:

> Of course this life here is not all battle, blood and sorrow. The colors and sounds of the earth are very sweet. . . . Human relationships bring satisfaction and pleasure beyond words. There are times when I feel that I never want to leave this place, no matter how beautiful and good heaven may be. But on the other hand, when I see more clearly the suffering of the race, . . . then the other side of the picture comes flooding in upon me. I realize that we have deep enjoyment only when we are successful in forgetting that even in our best moments countless others are suffering immeasurably.[3]

Suffering, of course, is not only the lot of "the world." Christians are not somehow immune to the struggle characterizing our age. Indeed, for the Christian the conflict is only accentuated, for loyalty to the king of the new age means living against the grain of the present. As Paul and Barnabas told new believers, "we must go through many hardships to enter the kingdom of God" (Acts 14:22).

Christians have at times attempted to deny this tension, to escape the problems associated with living under the demands of two kingdoms. Some have retreated from this world and have lived in solitude or in an environment secluded from the responsibilities of living in society. Others have compromised the radical claims of Jesus so as to make them less offensive to the prevailing norms of their own culture. Still others have compartmentalized their lives, attempting to live as though the kingdom of God were concerned only with spiritual matters and not with every segment of God's creation.

Such attempts notwithstanding, the message we hear from inspired men of old like John and Isaiah, Ezekiel and Jeremiah, is a call for absolute loyalty to the rule of God, now present in the world, regardless of personal cost.

5. Finally, the prophetic and apocalyptic Scriptures open our eyes to the reality of the future and its inseparable connection with the present. This is true in two ways. First, our present will not be forgotten with the coming of the kingdom. As Paul writes:

We boast about your perseverance and faith in all the persecutions and trials you are enduring.

All this is evidence that God's judgment is right, and as a result you will be counted worthy of the kingdom of God, for which you are suffering. God is just: He will pay back trouble to those who trouble you and give relief to you who are troubled, and to us as well. This will happen when the Lord Jesus is revealed from heaven in blazing fire with his powerful angels. He will punish those who do not know God and do not obey the gospel of our Lord Jesus. They will be punished with everlasting destruction and shut out from the presence of the Lord and from the majesty of his power on the day he comes to be glorified in his holy people and to be marveled at among all those who have believed. (2 Thess 1:4-10)

Thus are we taught that God is *not* mocked, after all. God's purpose and his people will be ultimately vindicated. There *will* be justice, as Malachi proclaims:

Who can endure the day of [the Lord's] coming? Who can stand when he appears? For he will be like a refiner's fire or a launderer's soap. He will sit as a refiner and purifier of silver; he will purify the Levites and refine them like gold and silver. . . .

"So I will come near to you for judgment. I will be quick to testify against sorcerers, adulterers and perjurers, against those who defraud laborers of their wages, who op-

press the widows and the fatherless, and deprive aliens of
justice, but do not fear me," says the LORD Almighty.
(3:2-5)

Second, our present is ultimately determined by the reality
of the future. God's future reign transforms and revolution-
izes the present. The new overlaps the old even now and will,
in a great act of God, decisively repudiate every aspect of
creaturely existence which opposes the kingdom of righteousness.[4]

These five affirmations, descriptive of the prophetic and
apocalyptic perspective, come together in what we today call
the Christian hope.[5] Their world view teaches us to look
"forward to a new heaven and a new earth, the home of righteousness" (2 Pet 3:13). They proclaim a new beginning (Jer
29; 31; Ezek 36; 37; Hos 2), when the conflict and tensions of
this age will be no more (Rev 21:4). This hope rests in divine
promise and is confirmed by Jesus' resurrection: God "has
given us new birth into a living hope through the resurrection
of Jesus Christ from the dead" (1 Pet 1:3; see also 1 Cor 15).
Moreover, our hope in the consummated kingdom is guaranteed by the present gift of the Spirit to all believers (Rom 5:5;
8:23-25; Eph 1:13-14).

But hope is not merely the certainty of God's instituting the
new age in Jesus' return, nor merely our expectant longing for
the liberating and transforming event. Rather, in the light of
what is to come we are to ask ourselves, What kind of people
ought we to be? (2 Pet 3:11). There is truth in Moltmann's description of the Christian church "as the community of those
who on the ground of the resurrection wait for the kingdom of
God *and whose life is determined by this expectation.*"[6]

Motivation for the Present

In many churches sermons on the fantastic portions of Revelation (that is, beyond chapter three) are few and far between. In
fact, I remember well the first such sermon I ever heard,

though the occasion was years ago. With great expense of
energy and artistic language, the preacher painted before
our eyes the great cosmic conflict, the heavenly warfare, so
that it seemed that the magnificent struggle must have been
going on right then and there. Then he drove home the point:
"In relation to the struggle of kingdom against kingdom," he
asked, "whose side are you on? What is your role in the battle?"

That sermon could have been evangelistic in purpose, calling unbelievers to join the army of God to struggle against the
kingdom of darkness. But it was not. It was a message directed
toward a community of believers who had forgotten that the
presence of the kingdom of God demands radical involvement. It was a powerful word to Christians who had neglected
the biblical witness, challenging the faithful to be awake and
ready for the unexpected intervention of God in bringing
this age to a close.

Under the threat of the promise of the coming kingdom,
the commencement of the Wedding Feast (see Rev 19:6-8),
many unworthy servants need to brush up their table man-
ners and dinner conversation.[7] The prophets and apocalyptists repeatedly accentuate our need to live in the light of
the promised future.

First, our hope in Christ spurs us on to *daily faithfulness*. In
chapter five we saw that the Hebrew prophets, by means of
threats and hopeful promises regarding the future, called
their people to daily renewal. Their word continues to speak
to us about our own lives, calling us to daily obedience. In the
same way, in response to the nearness of the kingdom, John
the Baptist told his audiences to "produce fruit in keeping
with repentance" (Mt 3:8).

Jesus' message also emphasizes the necessity of a life-chang-
ing response to the present and coming kingdom. Judgment
is imminent, and entry into the kingdom does not depend
on hearing Jesus' message or on fellowship with him, but
on repentance (Lk 13:22-30). In the Sermon on the Mount,

Jesus makes disturbingly clear that entrance into the kingdom will depend on daily obedience to the Father's will (Mt 7:21-23). Compared with the kingdom, all else is valueless; to discover it is to reorient one's whole life toward it (Mt 13:44-46). Life's only priority is kingdom seeking (Mt 6:33).[8]

Later writings in the New Testament only intensify and flesh out this call to daily faithfulness. In 2 Peter 3, we read: "In keeping with his promise we are looking forward to a new heaven and a new earth, the home of righteousness. So then, dear friends, since you are looking forward to this, make every effort to be found spotless, blameless and at peace with him" (vv. 13-14). Similarly, the author of 1 John writes: "Dear friends, now we are children of God, and what we will be has not yet been made known. But we know that when he appears, we shall be like him, for we shall see him as he is. Everyone who has this hope in him purifies himself, just as he is pure" (3:2-3).

In both instances the inspired writers draw a direct line from future to present: In light of what *will* happen, we should *now* be faithful. Because John knew the end of the time-long story—because he had read, as it were, the last chapter—he could encourage his people and write concerning present troubles: "This calls for patient endurance and faithfulness on the part of the saints" (Rev 13:10).

We have been discussing the present impact of the coming new age as though it were concerned only with our lives as individuals. Certainly, there is an important personal dimension to the promise of the kingdom of God. However, as the scope of God's reign extends beyond the individual, so our responsibility vis-à-vis the kingdom extends beyond personal faithfulness.

The inbreaking kingdom of God with its hope and promise of a new creation motivates us *to be a part of God's redemptive plan.* From time to time the Christian church is scandalized by the report of this sect or that community having withdrawn from

the world to await the return of Jesus. Having written off
the present age as hopeless, doomed to eternal destruction,
they have opted out of efforts toward influencing or transforming their worldly communities. This tendency may have
been present among the Thessalonian Christians (see 1 Thess
4:11-12; 5:14; 2 Thess 3:6-13). It could have been their emphat-
ic belief in the imminence of Jesus' return that was leading
them to idleness. However, the coming lordship of Christ
Jesus cannot be only hoped for and awaited. The expectation
of the Day of the Lord sets its stamp on our present calling
and mission.[9]

Against the backdrop of the Christian hope, the call to discipleship is a call to join in the work on behalf of the present
and coming kingdom of God. The task of the Christian community is to serve the purpose of God. And, as God's purpose
embraces all creation, so must our service extend to all creation. To take the prophetic and apocalyptic Scriptures seriously is to accept the inseparable connection between personal
spirituality and kingdom-work for this world. Personal devotion is meaningless, a sham, unless we

Stop doing wrong,
    learn to do right!
Seek justice,
    encourage the oppressed.
Defend the cause of the fatherless,
    plead the case of the widow. (Is 1:16-17)

What kind of devotion does God require? That which looses
the chains of injustice, sets the oppressed free, shares food with
the hungry, provides shelter for the homeless, clothes the
naked, and does not turn away one's own family (Is 58:6-7).
Jesus himself underscored this very message, teaching that
righteousness before God is seen in our commitment to serving the world (Mt 25:31-46).

The shape of Christian responsibility recalls the eschatological hope to which the prophets and apocalyptic writers

witnessed. Hope centered on a radically transformed world,
when

> The oppressor will come to an end,
>> and destruction will cease;
>> the aggressor will vanish from the land.
> In love a throne will be established;
>> in faithfulness a man will sit on it—
>> one from the house of David—
> one who in judging seeks justice
>> and speeds the cause of righteousness. (Is 16:4-5)

As in this well-known couplet from Amos—

> Let justice roll on like a river,
>> righteousness like a never-failing stream! (5:24)

—Isaiah testifies to a time of social justice, when righteousness will be the order of the day. Central to the message of the
later Hebrew prophets was the eschatological promise of
shalom—an all-embracing, everlasting salvation. This does not
mean merely personal morality, but the redemption of God's
creation, the accomplishment of his purpose.

In and through the church, and beyond, God is presently at
work bringing about his *shalom.*

Belief in the nearness of Jesus' return has characteristically
led to massive attempts at evangelization.[10] Indeed, a respon-
sible eschatology provides the cutting edge for the evangelistic message:

> To understand evangelism biblically ... is to see that in
> evangelism we are called to invite people to participate in a
> present reality, to respond to God's present working as well
> to his past acts, and to hope for the fulfillment of this pres-
> ent history in the future.[11]

The inbreaking kingdom of God demands a radical response
to the claims of Christ, and the Christian community is motivated by its hope to present that gospel.

As is evident from the scope of God's purpose, though,
evangelism is not the only way in which the church is to serve

the kingdom. Christians are also to share God's concern for justice and reconciliation throughout society. Christians are also to work with God against all forms of oppression, every manifestation of evil sundering human from human and human from God. The reign of Christ must be brought to bear on every aspect of existence. The kingdom of God is seen not only as God calls persons to repentance and faith but also as the standards of the kingdom—the ways of God—are established in the world.

The day is coming—it is upon us—when Christ shall return. His coming will fulfill the hope pervading the Bible, focused in the prophets. In the meantime, we live, like Daniel and his friends, hanging loosely on the world, knowing that our hope rests elsewhere, on the reign of God.

Notes

Chapter 2: Survey of Approaches to Interpretation
[1]See chapters seven and nine below.

[2]See also Stephen H. Travis, *I Believe in the Second Coming of Jesus* (Grand Rapids, Mich.: Eerdmans, 1982); Donald Guthrie, *New Testament Theology* (Downers Grove, Ill.: InterVarsity Press, 1981), pp. 791-818.

[3]Jesus foreshadowed this eschatological emphasis in his words at the Last Supper; see Mark 14:25. On the orientation of the Lord's Supper to the future in the practice of the early church, see I. Howard Marshall, *Last Supper and Lord's Supper* (Grand Rapids, Mich.: Eerdmans, 1980), especially pp. 152-53; and the more extensive *Eucharist and Eschatology* (London: Epworth Press, 1971) by Geoffrey Wainwright.

[4]In fact, the Greek transliteration of the Aramaic phrase here is ambiguous and could also mean "Our Lord has come." However, it is probable that Revelation 22:20 is a Greek translation of the same Aramaic expression, and in Revelation the reference is certainly to the future. Moreover, Paul already exhibits his expectation of the Lord's future coming in 1 Corinthians 11:26.

[5]According to a widely held view, this text employs traditional missionary terminology. See, for example, Leon Morris, *The Epistles of Paul to the Thessalonians* (Grand Rapids, Mich.: Eerdmans, 1956), p. 39.

[6]See, for example, the brief survey in I. Howard Marshall, *Biblical Inspiration* (Grand Rapids, Mich.: Eerdmans, 1982), pp. 75-93.

[7]Somewhat dated, but still useful, is the presentation of various points of view on a number of themes in R. Ludwigson, *A Survey of Biblical Prophecy* (Grand Rapids, Mich.: Zondervan, 1951).

[8]Herman A. Hoyt, "Dispensational Premillennialism," in *The Meaning of the Millennium: Four Views,* ed. Robert G. Clouse (Downers Grove, Ill.: Inter-

Varsity Press, 1977), pp. 66-67. See also Charles L. Feinberg, *Millennialism: The Two Major Views* (Chicago: Moody Press, 1936); J. Dwight Pentecost, *Things to Come: A Study in Biblical Eschatology* (Grand Rapids, Mich.: Zondervan, 1958); M. R. DeHaan, *Coming Events in Prophecy* (Grand Rapids, Mich.: Zondervan, 1962); Hal Lindsey, *The Late Great Planet Earth* (Grand Rapids, Mich.: Zondervan, 1970); *The 1980's: Countdown to Armageddon* (New York: Bantam Books, 1980); Tim LaHaye, *The Beginning of the End* (Wheaton, Ill.: Tyndale House, 1972).

[9]Lindsey, *The 1980's: Countdown to Armageddon*, p. xii. A critique of this procedure is given in John Goldingay, "The Old Testament and Christian Faith: Jesus and the Old Testament in Matthew 1—5," *Themelios* 8, no. 1 (September 1982): 4-10.

[10]Marshall, *Biblical Inspiration*, p. 84. Additional critiques are offered in George Eldon Ladd, *The New Testament and Criticism* (Grand Rapids, Mich.: Eerdmans, 1967); and Carl E. Armerding, *The Old Testament and Criticism* (Grand Rapids, Mich.: Eerdmans, 1983).

[11]Robert H. Mounce, *The Book of Revelation* (Grand Rapids, Mich.: Eerdmans, 1977), p. 12.

Chapter 3: Problems in Interpreting Biblical Prophecy

[1]Hal Lindsey's end-time schema suggests this very interpretation. See *The Late Great Planet Earth*, especially p. 54.

[2]In fact, some brushed-up reading skills would go far in driving away a herd of problems encountered in biblical interpretation. Among the relevant books is James W. Sire, *How to Read Slowly* (Downers Grove, Ill.: InterVarsity Press, 1978).

[3]"Rapture" is the English rendering of the Latin *rapere*, which translates the Greek *harpazō*. 1 Thessalonians 4:16-17 has been used as a proof-text for Jesus' catching up believers and returning with them to heaven. However, the nuance of "returning to heaven" is not present in the text. On the interpretation of the passage, see especially F. F. Bruce, *1 & 2 Thessalonians* (Waco, Tex.: Word, 1982), pp. 93-105.

[4]Some examples are given by Stephen Travis, *The Jesus Hope* (Downers Grove, Ill.: InterVarsity Press, 1974), pp. 85-86; and Robert G. Clouse, "The Danger of Mistaken Hopes," in *Handbook of Biblical Prophecy*, ed. Carl E. Armerding and W. Ward Gasque (Grand Rapids, Mich.: Baker Book House, 1977), pp. 27-39.

[5]Kenneth Scott Latourette, *A History of Christianity*, rev. ed., 2 vols. (New York: Harper & Row, 1975), 1:128-29.

[6]F. F. Bruce, *The Spreading Flame* (Grand Rapids, Mich.: Eerdmans, 1958), pp. 179-80.

[7]Travis, *The Jesus Hope*, p. 86.

[8]Lindsey, *The 1980's: Countdown to Armageddon*, p. xii.

[9]DeHaan, *Coming Events in Prophecy*, p. 15. See also Lindsey, *The Late Great Planet Earth*, p. 176; and Pentecost, *Things to Come*, pp. 9-33.

[10]Wolfhart Pannenberg effectively makes this point, though he fails to account for the risk involved in believing in the significance and historicity of events in the remote past (*Jesus–God and Man* [London: SCM, 1968], p. 110).

[11]As in LaHaye, *The Beginning of the End* (p. 8, for example), where to understand "Bible prophecy" seems equated with comprehending "clear events forecast in the Scriptures."

[12]Gordon D. Fee and Douglas Stuart, *How to Read the Bible for All Its Worth* (Grand Rapids, Mich.: Zondervan, 1981), p. 150.

[13]Donald Guthrie, *New Testament Introduction*, 3d ed. (Downers Grove, Ill.: InterVarsity Press, 1970), pp. 964-65.

Chapter 4: Prophecy as Scripture

[1]Among the scores of books written on this subject, these two are among the most helpful: R. C. Sproul, *Knowing Scripture* (Downers Grove, Ill.: InterVarsity Press, 1977), and the more advanced guide by Fee and Stuart, *How to Read the Bible for All Its Worth*. More academic is the volume edited by I. Howard Marshall, *New Testament Interpretation* (Grand Rapids, Mich.: Eerdmans, 1977).

[2]Here we part company with such writers as James M. Ward (*The Prophets* [Nashville: Abingdon, 1982], pp. 15-21) who, in the final analysis, are unwilling to admit for the Bible both human *and* divine authorship. On the topic of biblical inspiration, see Donald G. Bloesch, *Essentials of Evangelical Theology*, vol. 1: *God, Authority, and Salvation* (San Francisco: Harper & Row, 1978), chapter four; and Marshall, *Biblical Inspiration*.

[3]James W. Sire (*Scripture Twisting* [Downers Grove, Ill.: InterVarsity Press, 1980]) outlines some twenty types of interpretive errors to which the Bible has been subjected by various religious cults. Unfortunately, the flaws he presents are also to be found frequently within the Christian community.

[4]Fee and Stuart, *How to Read the Bible for All Its Worth*, p. 20.

[5]Of course, the distinction was only popularized, not invented, by Lindsey. "Literal" versus "allegorical" approaches to biblical interpretation have long been at the core of the debate over biblical prophecy. See Feinberg, *Millennialism*, pp. 37-66; and Pentecost, *Things to Come*, pp. 1-6, 16-64.

[6]Pentecost, *Things to Come*, p. 33.

[7]In Galatians 4:24, Paul employs a Greek word, *allēgoreō*, which means

"to speak allegorically." This passage is disputed, some scholars suggest
ing that Paul's "allegory" is really typology. (The distinction between these
two is made in chapter seven.) While Paul has begun with a historical
situation (as in typology), he goes on to find in the historical narrative
nidden and symbolic meanings (as in allegory). Another example of
Paul's use of allegory is in 1 Corinthians 9:9-10.

[8]See especially Richard N. Longenecker, *Biblical Exegesis in the Apostolic
Period* (Grand Rapids, Mich.: Eerdmans, 1975); also C. F. D. Moule,
The Birth of the New Testament, 3d ed. (San Francisco: Harper & Row,
1982), chapter four; C. K. Barrett, "The Interpretation of the Old
Testament in the New," in *The Authoritative Word*, ed. Donald K. McKim
(Grand Rapids, Mich.: Eerdmans, 1983), pp. 37-58.

[9]Lindsey, *The Late Great Planet Earth*, p. 173.

[10]Lindsey, *The 1980's: Countdown to Armageddon*, p. 89.

[11]Lindsey, *The Late Great Planet Earth*, pp. 105-6.

[12]A brief but helpful introduction to this area is the pamphlet by J. Stafford
Wright, *Interpreting the Bible* (Downers Grove, Ill.: InterVarsity Press,
1955). The volume by Fee and Stuart is built around the idea that different
biblical literary forms demand their own principles for interpretation.

[13]Sire, *Scripture Twisting*, pp. 51-52.

[14]DeHaan, *Coming Events in Prophecy*, p. 10.

[15]LaHaye, *The Beginning of the End*, pp. 91-93.

[16]An important matter we have not taken up is the difficulty in deciding
exactly what various authors mean by "literal interpretation." Ward
(*The Prophets*, p. 17) says that he intends to use a literal approach to the
Bible; for him this means ascertaining the meaning of the words as intended by the writers. However, interpreters like Lindsey and Pentecost
who also claim to use a literal approach would find little in Ward's writing
with which to agree. Because of this ambiguity I have opted not to use
the term at all. See, however, the well-balanced discussion in G. B. Caird,
The Language and Imagery of the Bible (London: Duckworth and Co. Ltd.,
1980), part two.

[17]It is notoriously difficult to recommend commentaries, not only because
of the sheer quantity of such works now available, but also because different commentaries are aimed at different readerships. The best schol-
arly commentary may be of little benefit to the general reader. A good, all-
purpose commentary set is the Tyndale series, available for the New Testament from Eerdmans and for the Old Testament from InterVarsity Press.
A series with some promise is The Bible Speaks Today, of which fourteen
volumes are now ready, published by InterVarsity Press. A more advanced, but not overly technical work is the New International Commen-

tary, Old and New Testaments, from Eerdmans. More advanced still are the Word Biblical Commentaries (Word Books), the New International Greek Text Commentary (Eerdmans) and the updated International Critical Commentary (T. & T. Clark), all in the process of being published. It should be added that commentary series are characteristically uneven in quality. Fee and Stuart give a beneficial discussion and suggested list of commentaries in *How to Read the Bible for All Its Worth*, pp. 219-24, though some of their selections are too technical for the general reader.

[18]*The New International Dictionary of New Testament Theology*, 3 vols. (Grand Rapids, Mich.: Zondervan, 1975-78), ed. Colin Brown, is an advanced, but extremely helpful tool for word study. Persons with even an elementary knowledge of Hebrew, or who can make use of the keys to Hebrew words in *Strong's Exhaustive Concordance*, may wish to consult the *Theological Wordbook of the Old Testament* (Chicago: Moody Press, 1980), ed. R. Laird Harris, Gleason L. Archer and Bruce K. Waltke.

[19]This study is concerned with the prophetic Scriptures. For a more general treatment see the books listed in note 1, chapter four.

Chapter 5: Prophecy as Genre

[1]Abraham is called a prophet in Genesis 20:7, but there the designation does not carry the special sense of one who communicates the word of God. As the mouthpiece of Moses (Ex 4:16), Aaron is also called a prophet (Ex 7:1).

The origins of Israel's prophetic tradition constitute a knotty problem. The relation of the prophets prior to the eighth century with those from the eighth century onward is also a matter of debate. As our main concern is the classical prophets, it will not be necessary here to engage in that discussion. See the introduction to the prophets of Israel in H. Alberto Soggin, *Introduction to the Old Testament* (Philadelphia: Westminster, 1976), pp. 211-23; and "nābî in the Old Testament" by Rolf Rendtorff, *Theological Dictionary of the New Testament*, 10 vols., ed. Gerhard Kittel and Gerhard Friedrich (Grand Rapids, Mich.: Eerdmans, 1964-76), 6:796-812.

[2]It can be argued that prophecy continued to play an important role in the Judaism of the Second Temple period, and there is some evidence in support of this view. However, if prophecy was alive and well during these years, it was in a form considerably different from that of classical prophecy as we know it from the Old Testament. Cf. Rudolf Meyer, "Prophecy and Prophets in the Judaism of the Hellenistic-Roman Period," in *Theological Dictionary of the New Testament*, 6:812-28; David E. Aune, *Prophecy in Early Christianity and the Ancient Mediterranean World*

(Grand Rapids, Mich.: Eerdmans, 1983), pp. 103-6.

[3]"In that Deuteronomy sees in the practices named here attempts to ascertain the will of the deity, it reaches the antithesis, splendid in its simplicity, between any mantic technique on the one hand and the prophetic office on the other. . . . It is now possible to sweep aside, as with a wave of the hand, the motley arsenal of mantic and occult practices, all the attempts to obtain a share of the divine powers or of divine knowledge. A quite different possibility has been disclosed to Israel, namely the Word of its prophet" (Gerhard von Rad, *Deuteronomy: A Commentary* [Philadelphia: Westminster, 1966], p. 123).

[4]A more developed mediatory role of the prophet is implied in Deuteronomy 18:16 and made explicit in such texts as Exodus 32:11-14, 30-32; Jeremiah 7:16; and Amos 7:1-6.

[5]Peter C. Craigie, *The Book of Deuteronomy* (Grand Rapids, Mich.: Eerdmans, 1976), p. 263.

[6]See Leonhard Goppelt, *Typos: The Typological Interpretation of the Old Testament in the New* (Grand Rapids, Mich.: Eerdmans, 1982), pp. 61-82. Speculation as to the relationship of the Prophet and the Messiah varied. Some expected only one person (see Jn 6:14-15). But John 7:40-41 indicates that others awaited a great prophet not identified with the Messiah. A differing, more complex view was held by the Jewish community at Qumran. Speaking in broad terms they awaited three messianic figures, one of whom was the Prophet. See Geza Vermes, *The Dead Sea Scrolls: Qumran in Perspective* (Philadelphia: Fortress, 1977), pp. 184-86.

[7]See John Bright, *A History of Israel,* 2d ed. (Philadelphia: Westminster, 1972), pp. 225-63. A brief introduction to "Prophecy in the Old Testament" is provided by Carl E. Armerding in *Handbook of Biblical Prophecy,* pp. 61-73.

[8]Bright, *A History of Israel,* p. 262. The relationship of prophet and covenant comes in for a more complete discussion in Douglas Stuart, "The Old Testament Prophets' Self Understanding of Their Prophecy," *Themelios* 6, no. 1 (September 1980): 9-14.

[9]The etymology of the Hebrew word for prophet is debated; however, the Greek term uses the preposition *pro* ("before"), used primarily in a local sense: "before" or "in front of" an assembly or person. Nevertheless, prophetic oracles at times included a temporal element, thus pointing to the predictive quality.

[10]That is, one must be suspicious of a writer who initiates a study on biblical prophecy with such a statement as: "The Hebrew prophets began predicting the pattern of future world events thousands of years ago" (Lindsey, *The 1980's: Countdown to Armageddon,* p. 11). This kind of interpre-

tive program fails to account for the *prophets'* main agenda—to call people in their own day to faithfulness.

[11]George Eldon Ladd, *The Presence of the Future* (Grand Rapids, Mich.: Eerdmans, 1974), pp. 64-65; cf. pp. 67-70. See also William Dyrness, *Themes in Old Testament Theology* (Downers Grove, Ill.: InterVarsity Press, 1979), pp. 223-24.

[12]See D. S. Russell, *The Method and Message of Jewish Apocalyptic* (London: SCM, 1964), pp. 73-82, who outlines the decline in prophecy and puts forward causal factors. See also Aune, *Prophecy in Early Christianity and the Ancient Mediterranean World*, pp. 110-14.

[13]Paul S. Minear, *New Testament Apocalyptic* (Nashville: Abingdon, 1981), p. 15. Identifying apocalyptic is a complex business. Good introductions are provided in Stephen H. Travis, *Christian Hope and the Future* (Downers Grove, Ill.: InterVarsity Press, 1980), pp. 25-40; Paul D. Hanson, "Apocalyptic, Genre," and "Apocalypticism," in *The Interpreter's Dictionary of the Bible,* Supplementary Volume, ed. Keith Crim (Nashville: Abingdon, 1976), pp. 27-28, 28-34, respectively; D. S. Russell, *Apocalyptic: Ancient and Modern* (London: SCM Press, 1978).

[14]See Travis, *Christian Hope and the Future,* pp. 25-40; as well as his "The Value of Apocalyptic," *Tyndale Bulletin* 30 (1979):53-76, which covers some of the same ground.

[15]For interpretive help, see especially Joyce G. Baldwin, *Daniel: An Introduction and Commentary* (Downers Grove, Ill.: InterVarsity Press, 1979).

[16]See the book-length discussion in *New Testament Apocalyptic* by Minear.

[17]See Travis, *Christian Hope and the Future,* pp. 41-49; and James D. G. Dunn, *Unity and Diversity in the New Testament* (Philadelphia: Westminster, 1977), pp. 318-22. Both Travis and Dunn point out apocalyptic features of Jesus' teaching.

[18]Our special concern is with prophecy in the early church; however, the ministry of John the Baptist is described after the manner of the Old Testament prophets. Jesus, too, can be seen, in part, in terms of the prophetic office. See Gerhard Friedrich, "Prophets and Prophecies in the New Testament," *Theological Dictionary of the New Testament,* 6:836-48. On the whole subject of prophecy in the New Testament, see David Hill, *New Testament Prophecy* (London: Marshall, Morgan and Scott, 1979); and the more technical, but authoritative work by Aune, *Prophecy in Early Christianity and the Ancient Mediterranean World.*

[19]See especially the commentary by G. R. Beasley-Murray, *The Book of Revelation* (Grand Rapids, Mich.: Eerdmans, 1974). Also, Michael Wilcock, *I Saw Heaven Opened: The Message of Revelation* (Downers Grove, Ill.: InterVarsity Press, 1975).

[20]See Beasley-Murray, *The Book of Revelation.*

Chapter 6: Symbolism: The Prophet's Tool

[1]J. R. R. Tolkien, *The Lord of the Rings,* vol. 3: *The Return of the King* (New York: Ballantine Books, 1965), p. 142.

[2]Revelation 13:1-3.

[3]Wilcock, *I Saw Heaven Opened,* pp. 24-25. Pentecost, *Things to Come* (pp. 39-44), recognizes the use of figurative language in the biblical writers to "embellish a language by adornment and to convey abstract ideas," but is of little help in discerning and explaining figurative language.

[4]See Ward, *The Prophets,* pp. 74-75.

[5]Particularly helpful here is Norman K. Gottwald, "Poetry, Hebrew," in *The Interpreter's Dictionary of the Bible,* 4 vols., ed. George Arthur Buttrick (Nashville: Abingdon, 1962), 3:829-38.

[6]So Sproul, *Knowing Scripture,* p. 99; Minear, *New Testament Apocalyptic,* p. 61; Pentecost, *Things to Come,* p. 55; et al.

[7]See Beasley-Murray, *The Book of Revelation.*

[8]Taken with Revelation 17:9, verse 18 can only refer to Rome (cf. Beasley-Murray, *The Book of Revelation,* pp. 260-61).

[9]Gordon D. Fee, *New Testament Exegesis* (Philadelphia: Westminster, 1983), p. 43.

[10]Cf. Beasley-Murray, *The Book of Revelation,* pp. 206-14.

[11]For a discussion of the symbolic use of numbers, see Marvin H. Pope, "Number, Numbering, Numbers," in *The Interpreter's Dictionary of the Bible,* 3, especially pp. 564-66.

[12]The problem of dating by numbers is effectively handled by Travis, *I Believe in the Second Coming of Jesus,* pp. 120-22. The interpretation of the thousand years (millennium) of Revelation 20 is an oft-discussed issue in Robert G. Clouse, ed., *The Meaning of the Millennium: Four Views* (Downers Grove, Ill.: InterVarsity Press, 1977).

Chapter 7: Prophecy and Jesus

[1]See the list of Old Testament prophecies concerning Christ and the church in Roger Nicole, "The Old Testament in the New Testament," in *The Expositor's Bible Commentary,* vol. 1, ed. Frank E. Gaebelein (Grand Rapids, Mich.: Zondervan, 1979), pp. 618-19.

[2]Cf. Goldingay, "The Old Testament and Christian Faith: Jesus and the Old Testament in Matthew 1—5. Part 1," pp. 4-10.

[3]Actually, no Old Testament prophecy states, "He will be called a Nazarene." One possible source is Isaiah 11:1, the prediction of a branch or shoot rising from the roots of Jesse. The Hebrew word used here, *neser,*

bears a phonetic similarity to that for *Nazarene;* furthermore, this verse in Isaiah was associated with messianic expectations. Another possibility is that Matthew was referring in general terms to Jesus' being scorned and rejected (Is 52:13—53:12), since Nazareth was a despised city (see Jn 1:46).

[4]Cf. Sigmund Mowinckel, *The Psalms in Israel's Worship,* 2 vols. in 1 (Nashville: Abingdon, 1962), 1:42-80.

[5]John Goldingay, *Approaches to Old Testament Interpretation* (Downers Grove, Ill.: InterVarsity Press, 1981), p. 117; cf. pp. 115-22. Cf. Leonhard Goppelt, *Theology of the New Testament,* 2 vols. (Grand Rapids, Mich.: Eerdmans, 1981-82), 2:56-57.

[6]Gerhard von Rad, *Old Testament Theology,* 2 vols. (New York: Harper & Row, 1962, 1965), 2:319. Cf. Gerhard F. Hasel, *Old Testament Theology: Basic Issues in the Current Debate,* rev. ed. (Grand Rapids, Mich.: Eerdmans, 1982), pp. 155-57.

[7]*Messiah* in the Old Testament is an adjective meaning "anointed," and was used to describe one set apart for specialized service to God. The word was especially employed in connection with kings (1 Sam 9:16; 24:6), since at his coronation the king was anointed with oil as a ritual of consecration.

[8]Geza Vermes (*Jesus the Jew* [London: Collins, 1973], p. 130) argues that the traditional Jewish view of the Messiah as King Messiah has often been blurred by modern attempts to deny the concept of Messiah any fixed content in intertestamental times. While it is true that certain Jewish sects and minorities had their own peculiar messianic speculations, it also remains apparent that the general hope of Palestinian Jewry centered on a King Messiah, Messiah Son of David. On the King Messiah, cf. Oscar Cullmann, *The Christology of the New Testament,* rev. ed. (Philadelphia: Westminster, 1959), pp. 113-17. For basic discussions of messianic expectation, see also D. S. Russell, *Between the Testaments* (Philadelphia: Fortress, 1960), pp. 119-29; and F. F. Bruce, *Jesus and Christian Origins Outside the New Testament* (Grand Rapids, Mich.: Eerdmans, 1974), pp. 66-81.

[9]Psalm of Solomon 17:23-36 (21-32).

[10]There is some debate about when the targums came to have a written form; hence, some might object to their being used as evidence for thought around the time of Christ. Yet, even if the evidence for an early date of writing is rejected, the targums nonetheless reflect earlier traditions. See Martin McNamara, *Targum and Testament* (Shannon, Ireland: Irish University Press, 1972).

[11]The proof-text collection is known as 4Q Testim and also includes references to a royal Messiah and a priest Messiah. An English translation of the anthology is given in G. Vermes, *The Dead Sea Scrolls in English* (New

York: Penguin Books, 1962), pp. 247-49. *The Rule of the Community* (1QS) is also found in English translation in Vermes, *The Dead Sea Scrolls in English*, pp. 71-94. The text here referred to is 1QS 9.11, which names the "Messiahs of Aaron and Israel"—the priestly and royal figures.

[12]A lengthy discussion of Jesus' use of messianic ideas is given in R. T. France, *Jesus and the Old Testament* (London: Tyndale Press, 1971; reprint ed., Grand Rapids, Mich.: Baker Book House, 1982), pp. 83-163. We will not open the Pandora's box of the problem of Jesus' messianic consciousness here; rather, we shall regard the Gospels as records enabling us to ascertain in a reliable way what Jesus thought of himself. See I. Howard Marshall, *I Believe in the Historical Jesus* (Grand Rapids, Mich.: Eerdmans, 1977).

[13]F. F. Bruce, *The New Testament Development of Old Testament Themes* (Grand Rapids, Mich.: Eerdmans, 1968), p. 90. Whether or not the identification of this text with the Servant was made in Judaism, it is nevertheless probable that it was made by the early church and by Jesus himself.

[14]Other illustrative texts include Mark 12:36; 14:27; and Luke 22:37.

[15]E. Earle Ellis, *Prophecy and Hermeneutic in Early Christianity* (Tübingen: J. C. B. Mohr, 1978), p. 165. The classic work on typology is Goppelt, *Typos: The Typological Interpretation of the Old Testament in the New*. See also D. L. Baker, *Two Testaments: One Bible* (Leicester: Inter-Varsity Press, 1976), chapter 6; and Goldingay, *Approaches to Old Testament Interpretation*, pp. 97-115.

[16]Bruce, *The New Testament Development of Old Testament Themes*, p. 21.

[17]Athanasius, "On the Incarnation," 34; in *Christology of the Later Fathers*, ed. Edward R. Hardy (Philadelphia: Westminster. 1954), pp. 87-88.

[18]von Rad, *Old Testament Theology*, 2:319. Cf. Martin Hengel, *The Atonement* (Philadelphia: Fortress, 1981), p. 59: "So far, then, we have no clear text from pre-Christian Judaism which speaks of the vicarious suffering of the Messiah in connection with Isa. 53." Lindsey (*The Late Great Planet Earth*, pp. 28-31) and Feinberg (*Millennialism*, p. 41) err in ascribing to pre-Christian Judaism a portrait of the suffering Messiah.

[19]Thus persons who, like Lindsey, take current events as their point of departure have doomed their interpretations from the outset. Further, the principle that the Old Testament must be interpreted in light of the New is additional evidence of the invalidity of a literalistic approach; taken literally, Isaiah 53 is not a reference to the coming Messiah.

Chapter 8: Prophecy Fulfilled

[1]Lindsey, *The 1980's: Countdown to Armageddon*, p. 86; cf. *The Late Great Planet Earth*, p. 20.

[2]"God's plan for Israel" will be discussed briefly in chapter nine.

[3]There is little to commend von Rad's suggestion that the promise in Deuteronomy was, from the outset, really concerned with the coming of an eschatological prophetic mediator (*Deuteronomy: A Commentary*, p. 123).

[4]France, *Jesus and the Old Testament*, p. 85.

[5]Pentecost, *Things to Come*, p. 93. Elsewhere Pentecost takes up the question of the conditional nature of prophecy, but concludes: "Prophecies based on unchanging covenants cannot admit the addition of any condition. Thus there is no warrant for assuming any conditions to the fulfillment of prophecy" (p. 49).

[6]Gordon J. Wenham, *The Book of Leviticus* (London: Hodder and Stoughton, 1979), p. 332.

[7]Gerhard F. Hasel, *Covenant in Blood* (Mountain View, Calif.: Pacific Press, 1982), p. 56. Hasel's book is noteworthy for its pervasive emphasis on the conditionality of this and other covenants. Cf. Goldingay, *Approaches to Old Testament Interpretation*, p. 121.

[8]Cf. Travis, *The Jesus Hope*, pp. 82-84.

[9]Helmut Thielicke, *The Evangelical Faith*, vol. 2: *The Doctrine of God and of Christ* (Edinburgh: T. & T. Clark, 1977), p. 360.

[10]Travis, *I Believe in the Second Coming of Jesus*, p. 140; cf. *The Jesus Hope*, pp. 82-83.

[11]Cf. Johannes Eichler, "Inheritance, Lot, Portion," in *The New International Dictionary of New Testament Theology*, 2:295-303.

[12]That the end is in view is indicated by the use of *synteleistha*, "to be consummated."

[13]Lindsey, *The 1980's: Countdown to Armageddon*, p. 20.

[14]Cf. Eduard Schweizer, *The Good News According to Mark* (Atlanta: John Knox, 1970), p. 269; George Bertram, "ὠδίν," in *Theological Dictionary of the New Testament*, 9:672-73.

[15]At the outset of his treatment of these signs, Lindsey laments: "The phenomena [Jesus] predicted just didn't seem all that phenomenal to me" (*The 1980's: Countdown to Armageddon*, p. 19). For a discussion of these signs and their manifestation in modernity, see Travis, *The Jesus Hope*, pp. 36-44.

[16]See Bruce (*1 & 2 Thessalonians*, pp. 179-88) for an extended and helpful excursus on the antichrist—including background, use in the New Testament and later developments. Also, see Erwin Kauder, "Antichrist," in *The New International Dictionary of New Testament Theology*, 1: 124-26; and I. Howard Marshall, *The Epistles of John* (Grand Rapids, Mich.: Eerdmans, 1978), pp. 148-51.

[17]On the problematic reference of 2:4 to God's temple, see I. Howard Mar-

shall, *1 and 2 Thessalonians* (Grand Rapids, Mich.: Eerdmans, 1983), pp.
190-92.
[18]Fee and Stuart, *How to Read the Bible for All Its Worth*, p. 217.

Chapter 9: Prophecy and God's Purpose

[1]For an informative, brief survey of the eschatological views of the Old
and New Testaments, see chapters 1 and 2 of Anthony A. Hoekema,
The Bible and the Future (Grand Rapids, Mich.: Eerdmans, 1979), pp.
3-22. As the future is not relegated to the last chapters of the Bible, so
"eschatology is not a mere appendage to the Christian faith" (James
Robert Ross, "Evangelical Alternatives," in *Handbook of Biblical Prophecy*,
p. 118).

One of the unfortunate fruits of much modern-day interest and writing
on "biblical prophecy" is the tendency to introduce an un- or antibiblical
dichotomy between God's purpose in creation and consummation. That
is, things concerning the end are pursued for their own sake, and not in
the total context of God's purpose. More on this will follow in this chapter
and the next.

[2]This concept of the *imago Dei* is founded on the biblical notion that God's
character is best described under the heading of "covenant love" (from
the Hebrew *ḥsd*). Covenant love transcends the obligatory; it entails
strength; it includes grace-favor without regard to merit. Covenant love
includes the righteousness motif and is fundamental to the idea of belong-
ing. It speaks of the attitude of, and action toward, solidarity. Covenant
love entails commitment, fellowship, faithfulness, steadfastness and
mercy. Therefore it is within God's own nature to reveal himself in word
and deed and to give himself in communion. On the idea of covenant
love, see von Rad, *Old Testament Theology*, 1:372; and Dyrness, *Themes
in Old Testament Theology*, pp. 57-60. On the human as God's covenant
partner, cf. Karl Barth, *Church Dogmatics* (Edinburgh: T. & T. Clark,
1975), III/1, pp. 183ff.

[3]Hasel, *Covenant in Blood*, p. 10.

[4]Helpful insight on the two kingdoms can be gained from Donald G.
Bloesch, *Essentials of Evangelical Theology*, vol. 2: *Life, Ministry, and Hope*,
pp. 131-54.

[5]On the Old Testament promise of the kingdom of God, see especially
Ladd, *The Presence of the Future*, pp. 45-75; also Dyrness, *Themes in Old
Testament Theology*, pp. 227-37.

[6]For discussions of the kingdom of God in New Testament thought, cf.
Ladd, *The Presence of the Future*, pp. 105-21; and Hoekema, *The Bible and
the Future*, pp. 41-54. Our own discussion also makes use of Karl Ludwig

Schmidt, "βασιλεία," in *Theological Dictionary of the New Testament,* 1:579-93.

[7]The verb used in Luke 7:16 is *episkeptomai,* one meaning of which signifies God's gracious visitation of humanity, employed here as a term with messianic import; see Exodus 4:31; Luke 1:68, 78; Hebrews 2:6. Cf. Hermann W. Beyer, "ἐπισκέπτομαι, ἐπισκοπέω," in *Theological Dictionary of the New Testament,* 2:603-5.

[8]I. Howard Marshall, *Pocket Guide to Christian Beliefs,* 3d ed. (Downers Grove, Ill.: InterVarsity Press, 1978), p. 129.

[9]Ladd, *The Presence of the Future,* p. 218; see also p. 307.

[10]For example, DeHaan, *Coming Events in Prophecy,* p. 93. Philip Edgcumbe Hughes (*Interpreting Prophecy: An Essay in Biblical Perspectives* [Grand Rapids, Mich.: Eerdmans, 1976]) presents a helpful discussion which accounts more fully for the witness of the New Testament. See also the chapter on "Prophecy and Fulfillment: The Last Days," in Carl F. H. Henry, *God, Revelation and Authority: God Who Speaks and Shows* (Waco Tex.: Word, 1979), 3:20-27.

[11]For example, LaHaye, *The Beginning of the End.*

[12]This is the interpretation offered by "dispensationalists," the most well-known of whom is Hal Lindsey. See his writings along with those of DeHaan, LaHaye, Pentecost and Feinberg. For critiques of this interpretation, see especially Hughes, *Interpreting Prophecy;* Hoekema, *The Bible and the Future,* pp. 194-222; Philip Mauro, *The Hope of Israel* (Swengel, Penn.: Reiner Publications, n.d.); and the exchange in Clouse, ed., *The Meaning of the Millennium.*

[13]Literally, these words mean "assembly," "gathering" or "congregation." However, the real point in their usage when describing the "assembly of God" is to indicate *who* assembles, or *who* constitutes the assembly. Cf. Karl L. Schmidt, "ἐκκλησία" in *Theological Dictionary of the New Testament,* 3:527.

[14]See Ladd, *The Presence of the Future,* pp. 262-77; Hans Küng, *The Church* (Garden City, N. Y.: Image, 1976), pp. 124-44; and Howard A. Snyder, *Liberating the Church: The Ecology of Church and Kingdom* (Downers Grove, Ill.: InterVarsity Press, 1983).

[15]Contrary to Hughes, *Interpreting Prophecy,* p. 107: "If there is a difference between the 'kingdom' and the 'church,' the apostles and evangelists of the New Testament seem to have been unaware of it." DeHaan (*Coming Events in Prophecy,* p. 61) finds fault with those who "spiritualize" God's promises to Israel by associating them with the church. This, he asserts, is tantamount to equating "church" and "kingdom." DeHaan fails to notice that it is the New Testament which applies Israel's promises to the

church. Moreover, he himself is guilty of equating "Israel" and "kingdom"—a nonbiblical concept. Both Hughes and DeHaan mistakenly assume that God's kingdom refers to a sphere of rule, rather than to God's dynamic rule itself.

[16]Küng, *The Church*, p. 131.

[17]Barth, *Church Dogmatics*, IV/3, 2:762.

[18]Shirley C. Guthrie, *Christian Doctrine: Teachings of the Christian Church* (Atlanta: John Knox, 1968), p. 398.

Chapter 10: The Prophetic Message

[1]For example, Waldron Scott, *Bring Forth Justice* (Grand Rapids, Mich.: Eerdmans, 1980); Ronald J. Sider, *Rich Christians in an Age of Hunger* (Downers Grove, Ill.: InterVarsity Press, 1977).

[2]On the affirmations to follow, see J. Andrew Kirk, *Theology Encounters Revolution* (Downers Grove, Ill.: InterVarsity Press, 1980), chapter nine; James Robert Ross, "Living Between Two Ages," in *Handbook of Biblical Prophecy*, pp. 231-41; Hoekema, *The Bible and the Future*, chapter six; Travis, *I Believe in the Second Coming of Jesus*, chapter seven.

[3]Charles Durham, *Temptation: Help for Struggling Christians* (Downers Grove, Ill.: InterVarsity Press, 1982), p. 157.

[4]Kirk, *Theology Encounters Revolution*, pp. 166-67; Jürgen Moltmann, *Theology of Hope* (New York: Harper & Row, 1967), pp. 15-16.

[5]See Richard N. Longenecker, "The Return of Christ," in *Handbook of Biblical Prophecy*, pp. 143-63; Travis, *I Believe in the Second Coming of Jesus, The Jesus Hope, Christian Hope and the Future;* Ernst Hoffmann, "Hope, Expectation," in *The New International Dictionary of New Testament Theology*, 2:238-46.

[6]Moltmann, *Theology of Hope*, p. 326 (italics mine).

[7]David Lowes Watson, "Evangelism and Missions: A Survey of Recent Books (Part III)," *TSF Bulletin* 5, no. 3 (January/February 1982):17.

[8]In the saying "But seek first his kingdom and his righteousness . . . ", "first" should not be understood sequentially, as though Jesus were giving only the first of a list of priorities. On the contrary, he was calling on all persons to give their whole lives to serving the kingdom of God.

[9]Moltmann, *Theology of Hope*, pp. 329-30; see C. René Padilla, ed., *The New Face of Evangelicalism* (Downers Grove, Ill.: InterVarsity Press, 1976), chapters five and fifteen; Travis, *I Believe in the Second Coming of Jesus*, pp. 235-50; Ross, "Living between Two Ages," pp. 235-41; Ronald J. Sider, ed., *Evangelicals and Development: Toward a Theology of Social Change* (Philadelphia: Westminster, 1981), especially chapter three.

[10]Donald W. Dayton (*Discovering an Evangelical Heritage* [New York:

Harper & Row, 1976], pp. 126-27) notes how the rise of premillennialism resulted in the decline of social involvement among evangelical Christians.

[11] Alfred C. Krass, *Five Lanterns at Sundown: Evangelism in a Chastened Mood*
(Grand Rapids, Mich.: Eerdmans, 1978), p. 67. Krass's study is notable
for its explication of the evangelistic task and message in the context of
the inbreaking kingdom of God.

Glossary

allegory: A method of interpretation in which special, hidden meanings are attached to the details of an event or text without regard for the historical context of that event or text.

apocalypse: A transliteration of the Greek *apocalypsis,* meaning "revelation" or "disclosure." The term is also used to denote literary compositions which resemble the book of Revelation.

apocalyptic: 1. A distinctive *literary genre* in which the author communicates a message from God by means of narrating both the visions he has presumably experienced and their interpretation. 2. A *religious perspective* focusing especially on the imminent intervention of God into worldly affairs to bring to an end the present evil age and usher in the ideal age of salvation. 3. A *religiously charged social setting* in which an alienated, despairing people refocus life to minimize the significance of the present, worldly ambiguities and inequities, and maximize the significance of what God is doing on a cosmic level to bring about salvation and deliverance. See pp. 61-65 in the text.

Aramaic: One of the Semitic languages, related to Hebrew. It was the primary language spoken in Palestine in Jesus' day.

consummation: The climax and completion of God's eternal purpose for his creation.

eschatological: An adjective describing things, events, persons, etc., having to do with the last days and the inbreaking of God's rule over all the earth.

eschatology: Literally, the doctrine or study of the last things.

genre: A literary form or kind of writing—for example, "autobiography" or "historical novel."

Messiah: A transliteration of the Hebrew word for "anointed one." In Greek the equivalent is "Christ."

millennium: Literally, a thousand-year reign, from the Latin *mille*, "a thousand," and *annus*, "year." A technical term for the thousand-year reign of Christ in Revelation 20:1-6. There are three basic views for how the millennial reign of Christ will be realized:
 1. amillennialism: The view that the millennial reign of Christ is now in process of being realized.
 2. premillennialism: The view that the millennial reign of Christ will be preceded by the Second Coming of Christ.
 3. postmillennialism: The view that the present age will gradually merge into the millennial reign of Christ as Christianity gains in its worldwide influence.
(See further, the suggested reading list under "Issues in the Interpretation of Biblical Prophecy.")

parousia: A transliteration of the Greek *paroysia*, meaning "coming" or "being present." The word is used as a technical term for the Second Coming of Christ.

prediction: A statement which looks forward to and demands its fulfillment in a future, historical event or person.

Qumran community: An esoteric, highly disciplined, Jewish sect which withdrew into the desert from public life in order to maintain moral and religious purity and prepare for the final battle against the Children of Darkness. They maintained a critical stance toward mainstream Judaism.

targums: Translations of the Hebrew Scriptures into Aramaic, the vernacular of most Palestinians. Before reaching written form, these translations were given orally in the synagogues.

typology: A method of interpretation in which a current event, person, etc., is viewed against the pattern of a corresponding past, historical event, person, etc. Thus the exodus from Egypt is viewed as a type of the Christians' deliverance from the bondage of sin.

Suggested Reading

Unmarked titles are appropriate for general readers. Asterisked (*) titles are for those desiring a more advanced and technical discussion.

The Character and Interpretation of the Bible
*Armerding, Carl E. *The Old Testament and Criticism.* Grand Rapids, Mich.: Eerdmans, 1983.

Fee, Gordon D., and Douglas Stuart. *How to Read the Bible for All Its Worth.* Grand Rapids, Mich.: Zondervan, 1981.

*Goldingay, John. *Approaches to Old Testament Interpretation.* Downers Grove, Ill.: InterVarsity Press, 1981.

*Ladd, George Eldon. *The New Testament and Criticism.* Grand Rapids, Mich.: Eerdmans, 1967.

Marshall, I. Howard. *Biblical Inspiration.* Grand Rapids, Mich.: Eerdmans, 1982.

Sproul, R. C. *Knowing Scripture.* Downers Grove, Ill.: InterVarsity Press, 1977.

Prophecy and Prophets in the Old and New Testaments
*Aune, David E. *Prophecy in Early Christianity and the Ancient Mediterranean World.* Grand Rapids, Mich.: Eerdmans, 1983.

Dyrness, William. *Themes in Old Testament Theology.* Downers Grove, Ill.: InterVarsity Press, 1979.

*Hill, David. *New Testament Prophecy.* Atlanta: John Knox, 1979.

Ward, James M. *The Prophets.* Nashville: Abingdon, 1982.

Apocalyptic in Biblical and Intertestamental Literature
*Aune, David E. *Prophecy in Early Christianity and the Ancient Mediterranean*

World. Grand Rapids, Mich.: Eerdmans, 1983.

Hanson, Paul D. "Apocalypticism." In *The Interpreter's Dictionary of the Bible.* Supplementary Volume, pp. 28-34. Edited by Keith Crim. Nashville: Abingdon, 1976.

Minear, Paul S. *New Testament Apocalyptic.* Nashville: Abingdon, 1981.

Russell, D. S. *Apocalyptic: Ancient and Modern.* London: SCM Press Ltd., 1978.

*Travis, Stephen H. *Christian Hope and the Future.* Downers Grove, Ill.: InterVarsity Press, 1980.

Jesus as the Fulfillment of Prophecy

*Bruce, F. F. *The New Testament Development of Old Testament Themes.* Grand Rapids, Mich.: Eerdmans, 1968.

*France, R. T. *Jesus and the Old Testament.* Grand Rapids, Mich.: Baker Book House, 1982.

Issues in the Interpretation of Biblical Prophecy

Armerding, Carl E., and W. Ward Gasque, eds. *Handbook of Biblical Prophecy.* Grand Rapids, Mich.: Baker Book House, 1977.

Clouse, Robert G., ed. *The Meaning of the Millennium: Four Views.* Downers Grove, Ill.: InterVarsity Press, 1977.

Hoekema, Anthony A. *The Bible and the Future.* Grand Rapids, Mich.: Eerdmans, 1979. *(Amillennial position)*

Hughes, Philip Edgcumbe. *Interpreting Prophecy.* Grand Rapids, Mich.: Eerdmans, 1976. *(Amillennial position)*

Pentecost, J. Dwight. *Things to Come.* Grand Rapids, Mich.: Zondervan, 1958. *(Dispensational Premillennial position)*

*Travis, Stephen H. *Christian Hope and the Future.* Downers Grove, Ill.: InterVarsity Press, 1980.

Travis, Stephen H. *I Believe in the Second Coming of Jesus.* Grand Rapids, Mich.: Eerdmans, 1982.

On Constructing a Biblical Eschatology

*Berkouwer, G. C. *The Return of Christ.* Grand Rapids, Mich.: Eerdmans, 1972.

*Ladd, George Eldon. *The Presence of the Future.* Grand Rapids, Mich.: Eerdmans, 1974.

Travis, Stephen H. *I Believe in the Second Coming of Jesus.* Grand Rapids, Mich.: Eerdmans, 1982.